MOSCOW
AND BEYOND

MOSCOW AND BEYOND

1986 to 1989

Andrei Sakharov

TRANSLATED BY ANTONINA BOUIS

VINTAGE BOOKS

A DIVISION OF RANDOM HOUSE, INC.

NEW YORK

FIRST VINTAGE BOOKS EDITION, APRIL 1992

Copyright © 1990 by Alfred A. Knopf, Inc.

All rights reserved under International and Pan-American Copyright
Conventions. Published in the United States by Vintage Books, a division
of Random House, Inc., New York, and simultaneously in Canada by
Random House of Canada Limited, Toronto. Originally published in
Russian as *Gorkii, Moskva, dalee vezde* by Chekhov Publishing
Corporation. Copyright © by Chekhov Publishing Corporation. This
translation first published in hardcover in the United States by
Alfred A. Knopf, Inc., New York, in 1990.

Library of Congress Cataloging-in-Publication Data
Sakharov, Andreĭ, 1921–
[Gor 'kiĭ, Moskva, dalee vezde. English]
Moscow and beyond, 1986 to 1989/Andrei Sakharov; translated by
Antonina Bouis.—1st Vintage Books ed.
p.   cm.
Translation of: Gor 'kiĭ, Moskva, dalee vezde.
Originally published: 1st American ed. New York: Knopf, 1991.
Includes index.
ISBN 0-679-73987-4
1. Sakharov, Andreĭ, 1921–1989.   2. Dissenters—Soviet Union—
Biography.   3. Human rights workers—Soviet Union—Biography.
4. Soviet Union—Politics and government—1985-   .   I. Title.
[DK275.S25A3   1992b]
323'.092—dc20
[B]   91-50700
CIP

Manufactured in the United States of America
10   9   8   7   6   5   4   3   2   1

CONTENTS

16 pages of photos follow page 106

FOREWORD

I consider democracy the only satisfactory road for a country's development. The centuries-old servile Russian spirit, combined with our suspicion of foreigners and their ideas, seems to me a terrible affliction, not a sign of national vitality. Only democratic institutions can mature the national character and enable it to deal soundly with our ever more complicated world.

—Andrei Sakharov, 1974

ON DECEMBER 23, 1986, as he stepped off the train at Moscow's Yaroslavl Station to face a crowd of eager correspondents from all over the world, Andrei Sakharov, the Soviet Union's most celebrated dissenter, was sixty-five years old, his health badly undermined by hunger strikes and heart disease. For the past seven years he had been confined to the city of Gorky, banished from Moscow for his outspoken opposition to the war in Afghanistan. In a letter to Gorbachev, written prior to his release from exile, he had stated his intention to devote himself to science and private life, to minimize his public activities, to speak out only in exceptional circumstances when his conscience would not let him remain silent. Some reporters speculated that he would now shun politics entirely, while others thought his reputation might be used—or abused—to gain international acceptance for Gorbachev's "new thinking." What no one anticipated was that Sakharov would marshal his will, his intelligence, and his moral authority to set a new national agenda and prepare the way for parliamentary democracy in the Soviet Union.

Moscow and Beyond, the second (and much briefer) volume of Andrei Sakharov's autobiography, covers the period from December 1986 through his participation in the June 1989 Congress of People's Deputies—thirty eventful months that transformed the political structure of the Soviet Union.*

In *Memoirs,* the first volume published earlier this year, Sakharov describes his upbringing in a traditional Russian intelligentsia family; his studies at Moscow University, followed by wartime service as an engineer-inventor at a munitions factory; his twenty years spent as the Soviet Union's foremost thermonuclear weapons scientist; his contributions to controlled fusion reactions, to cosmology, and to elementary particle physics; his campaign to limit nuclear testing, which brought him into conflict with Soviet officials; the worldwide publication of his 1968 essay *Reflections on Progress, Peaceful Coexistence, and Intellectual Freedom;* the death of his first wife and his marriage in 1972 to Elena Bonner; his years at the center of the human rights movement, defending individual victims of political repression; the award to him of the 1975 Nobel Peace Prize; his exile to Gorky; and, finally, Gorbachev's phone call inviting him to return to Moscow and to resume his "patriotic work." In his review of the *Memoirs,* Ernest Gellner wrote in the *Times Literary Supplement* that "the life of Andrei Sakharov is probably *the* life of the

---

Moscow and Beyond is a firsthand and distinctively personal account of the revolutionary ferment in the Soviet Union during the period in question; it is not, and was never intended to be, a comprehensive history of *perestroika.* For readers who wish to delve further, Leonard Schapiro's *The Communist Party of the Soviet Union* (second edition, Vintage Books, 1971) remains the classic study of pre-Gorbachev Soviet politics; Geoffrey Hosking's *The Awakening of the Soviet Union* (Harvard University Press, 1990) lucidly describes the historical and social roots of current reforms; *Voices of Glasnost* (Stephen Cohen and Katrina vanden Heuvel, Norton, 1989) contains informative interviews with Alexander Yakovlev, Yuri Afanasiev, Evgeny Velikhov, and other Moscow liberals; Anders Åslund's *Gorbachev's Struggle for Economic Reform* (Cornell University Press, 1989) offers an informed analysis of Soviet economic issues; *Soviet Disunion* (Bohdan Nahaylo and Victor Swoboda, Free Press, 1990) is a useful if sometimes tendentious survey of the nationalities problem; and Strobe Talbott's *The Master of the Game* (Alfred A. Knopf, 1988) is a readable history of nuclear arms control, which gives Sakharov proper credit (pp. 358–61) for helping to break the deadlock over the Strategic Defense Initiative in February 1987.

age; he lived the triumph of physics *and* the catastrophe of Marxism.
. . . I doubt whether any other single book has conveyed so vividly, so
many-sidedly, and (I believe) so accurately, the realities and options of
Soviet life and sensibility over the past half-century."

Gorbachev's phone call to Sakharov—together with his dispatch of
the president of the Academy of Sciences to brief Sakharov in Gorky on
the status of disarmament negotiations—was recognized, even at the
time, as something more than a show of personal favor or a concession
to Western public opinion. Gorbachev was seeking to overcome the
persistent hostility between state and society that has deformed Russia's
political history. That country's rulers, both tsars and commissars, have
traditionally viewed the people as subjects, not citizens, and the people,
both the common man and the intelligentsia, have reciprocated by
regarding the state as the enemy, as "them" instead of "us."

WHEN GORBACHEV was elected General Secretary of the Communist
Party in March 1985, he apparently still believed that the Soviet economy could be reinvigorated by simply eliminating the corruption and
obvious deficiencies of the Brezhnev regime. Those promoted to top
posts in 1985 and 1986—Ligachev, Ryzhkov, Chebrikov, Zaikov, Yeltsin, Talyzin, Slyunkov—were mainly successful *apparatchiki*, many
with backgrounds in the military-industrial complex. In a major speech
on restructuring the economy delivered in June 1985, Gorbachev put in
first place the goal of "increasing the efficiency of centralism in management and planning." Production discipline was tightened. Superminis-
tries were established to control agriculture and construction. Cam-
paigns were launched against alcoholism and against "unearned
incomes."

The terrifying accident at the Chernobyl nuclear power plant in April
1986, exposing millions of people to dangerous levels of radiation and
causing billions of rubles of damage, seems to have convinced Gorbachev
that more efficient management would not be sufficient, and that he
would have to look beyond the *apparat* and the intellectual establishment if he wanted to develop a reform program capable of curing the
country's ills. Egor Yakovlev was named editor of *Moscow News*, Vitaly
Korotich of *Ogonyok*, Sergei Zalygin of *Novy Mir*, and Grigory Baklanov
of *Znamya*. In conjunction with this extension of *glasnost*, Gorbachev's

overture to Sakharov, in effect accepting him as the government's loyal opposition, made plain that Gorbachev intended *perestroika* to be something more than the futile tinkering with the system which had been attempted intermittently since Stalin's death. As it turned out, notwithstanding some disturbing zigzags, Gorbachev has since adopted Sakharov's own long-term goal for his country—an open society based on democratic institutions, the Rule of Law, and rapprochement with the West. He has also followed many specific recommendations of Sakharov's that when first proposed seemed like naïve fantasies: the release of prisoners of conscience; an end to the jamming of foreign broadcasts; withdrawal from Afghanistan; adoption of a law regulating the secession of Union Republics; abolition of the Communist Party's political monopoly; and much else besides.

SAKHAROV WAS certainly not alone in criticizing the Soviet system in the 1960s and 1970s. Dissenters inside the establishment now and then managed to slip past the censor an oblique complaint about the state of affairs, although for the most part they were biding their time in academic institutes, "mired in shit," as historian Yuri Afanasiev bluntly put it. Alexander Yesenin-Volpin, Valery Chalidze, Andrei Amalrik, Pavel Litvinov, Larisa Bogoraz, Sergei Kovalev, Yuri Orlov, and other courageous dissidents went further and openly challenged Soviet misdeeds and insisted—before they were imprisoned or sent into exile—that respect for human rights was a prerequisite for the revival of civil society. Roy Medvedev became the leading proponent of socialist democracy, and Alexander Solzhenitsyn called for a return to traditional Russian religious and political values. And yet, while all these individuals played significant roles in preparing the way for *perestroika,* the paramount figure was unquestionably Sakharov. His persistent dedication to truth in the face of government denunciation, his freedom from bitterness or personal political ambition, his tireless efforts on behalf of individual victims of oppression, won him the unrivaled respect of the intelligentsia and later, after Soviet television made him known throughout the USSR, the general public as well. In a poll taken shortly after his death, Sakharov was named the most revered figure in Soviet history, edging out Lenin— Gorbachev, Yeltsin, and other notables all trailed some distance behind. The choice of Sakharov as their hero suggests that the Russian people are better prepared for democracy than conventional wisdom has supposed.

Moscow and Beyond includes observations on the places Sakharov visited and the people he saw in November and December 1988 during his first-ever trip abroad. He possessed the faculty of viewing the world with a child's freshness of vision, free of prejudices and preconceptions; this, coupled with his critical intelligence, makes his remarks thought-provoking on topics ranging from the Cathedral of Notre Dame to the bureaucratic ways of American philanthropic foundations. This volume also continues the story of his intimate and multifaceted relationship with Elena Bonner. But for the most part, it chronicles his growing absorption in politics—at first focusing on his own special issues of amnesty for prisoners of conscience and nuclear disarmament,* then on ethnic conflict in Armenia, Georgia, and Azerbaijan, election contests in the Academy of Sciences and the city of Moscow, and finally participation in the First Congress of People's Deputies, where as prophet, gadfly, and loyal opposition he prodded Gorbachev to accelerate the pace of reform.

Sakharov's account of the Congress, which met in Moscow from May 25 to June 9, 1989, underscores its decisive impact on the course of Soviet politics and explains why it irreversibly altered the nature of the Soviet Union. For two weeks, the whole country watched in fascination as economists, farmers, generals, doctors, bureaucrats, miners, and scientists offered firsthand uncensored testimony about conditions and events in Moscow, Tbilisi, Sverdlovsk, and cities and hamlets scattered across the USSR. The deputies did not—and could not—exercise direct power and solve the problems they had uncovered, but they magnificently fulfilled at least one of a parliament's essential roles, that of informing

---

*In December 1986, during his brief phone conversation with Gorbachev, Sakharov stressed that the release of prisoners of conscience was a priority for him; over the next few months several hundred were freed from labor camps and psychiatric hospitals, and prosecutions under the "political" articles of the Criminal Code came to a virtual halt. In February 1987, two weeks after Sakharov's public criticism of Soviet linkage of nuclear disarmament to U.S. abandonment of the Strategic Defense Initiative, Gorbachev offered to negotiate limits on Soviet and U.S. intermediate-range missiles in Europe separately from all other issues, a breakthrough that led to the elimination of a whole class of nuclear weapons.

the public and stimulating debate. The Congress transformed a nation of subjects into a nation of citizens.

AT THE CONGRESS, Sakharov declined nomination to serve in the Supreme Soviet—he believed that its members should become full-time legislators, and he was not yet prepared to commit himself totally to politics. He did, however, accept appointment to the commission created to draft a new constitution, and he was also elected to the five-member governing board of the Interregional Group of Deputies, a parliamentary caucus of reformers.*

In June 1989, after the close of the Congress, Sakharov traveled to England to receive an honorary degree from Oxford University, and then continued on to the United States, where he completed work on his *Memoirs* and on the present work. In late August, after a one-week vacation in the south of France, he returned to Moscow.

While he was abroad, I asked Sakharov why he had abandoned his resolve to concentrate on science. His response was simple and direct: after weighing his current capabilities and the country's needs, he felt that he could make a greater contribution to politics than to physics. He made plain that he well understood his power to stimulate discussion and to influence the shape of the emerging political order; he was aware of his limits as well, and was ready to let experts like Nikolai Shmelyov and Nikolai Petrakov elaborate detailed guidelines for the reforms he proposed, and professional politicians like Gorbachev and Yeltsin implement them.

---

*Outsiders are often confused by the press's habit of referring to members of the Interregional Group as "left radicals." Deputies in the Group, notwithstanding differences on particular points, basically support multiparty parliamentary democracy and safeguards for civil and political rights; with various reservations, they advocate free enterprise, including a market economy and private property, and local autonomy. "Conservatives" in current Soviet terminology favor comprehensive central administration and usually assign a commanding role to the Communist Party. If the coloration given the terms by recent Western politics is ignored, the dictionary definition of "radical" as "advocating sweeping changes in laws and methods of government with the least delay" seems appropriate, as does the original usage of "left" to denote an individual not bound by orthodox tenets of political philosophy, and favoring democratic or republican, as distinguished from monarchical or aristocratic, forms of governance.

Back in Moscow, contrary to his earlier intention, he faithfully attended sessions of the Supreme Soviet, which met from September 25 through November 29, frequently entering into the debates. At one memorable session, when the Supreme Soviet was on the verge of granting Gorbachev sweeping and ill-defined emergency powers, Sakharov stood up and singlehandedly persuaded the assembly to defer final passage of the bill for twenty-four hours. The amended version adopted the next day included additional safeguards designed to deter arbitrary action, while still giving the chief executive the necessary authority to deal promptly with authentic crises.

On weekends and evenings Sakharov would attend meetings of the Memorial Society and other civic associations and patiently sit through the tedious speech-making, mindful that his presence on the dais provided tangible encouragement to rank-and-file members. He personally escorted Vorkuta miners around Moscow in search of a lawyer who would plead their cause. He traveled to Chelyabinsk to speak at a ceremony commemorating Stalin's victims.

And he continued to work on an outline for a new constitution. Sakharov's preliminary draft, completed only a few days before his death, provides for a Union government consisting of a bicameral Congress of People's Deputies; a President chosen for a five-year term through a direct, competitive, popular election; a Council of Ministers; and a Supreme Court. Asserting that individuals and commercial corporations should enjoy the right to own property and compete with state enterprises on an equal footing, he calls for a mixed market economy, with government intervention limited to those measures needed to secure the general welfare and create a social safety net.

Sakharov devotes particular attention to relations between the constituent entities of the present Union of Soviet Socialist Republics and of the "Union of Soviet Republics of Europe and Asia," his suggested name for the future federation. Lubomyr Hajda and Mark Beissinger have stated the basic dilemma facing such a multinational state:

Gorbachev came to power with the idea of modernizing the Soviet empire in order to maintain it; within several years' time, his thinking had evolved to the position that the empire should be transcended without being dissolved, that it was necessary to move beyond empire without surrendering the *imperium*. This meant

turning an odd and involuntary conglomeration of nations, united
only by their common experience of Russian imperial domination,
into a consensual and voluntary union. History not only gives no
precedents for such a transformation; it suggests the idea itself is
utopian.*

Sakharov did not pretend to have devised a definitive solution of the
nationalities issue, which has come to dominate so many facets of the
Soviet political system. But his constitution at the very least provides
some signposts. The USSR's Union Republics and autonomous regions
would be given the choice of either acceding to a new Union treaty or
declaring their independence; the decision would be made by the appropriate legislative body. All those that joined the new Union would be
granted equal status as republics, and their currently existing borders
would be guaranteed for ten years; after that, they could be adjusted by
means of arbitration in accordance with the principle of self-determina-
tion. The central Union government would be responsible for defense,
foreign affairs, the monetary system, the nationwide transportation and
communications systems, and other matters specifically delegated to it
by the republics. The rights enumerated in the Constitution and in the
International Covenants on Human Rights would be guaranteed
throughout the Union, and discrimination on the basis of nationality,
religious belief, or political opinion would be prohibited.

Sakharov sought in his draft constitution to put into concrete, practical terms for the future Soviet Union the vision of a "flexible, pluralist,
tolerant society" set forth in his Nobel lecture, "Peace, Progress, and
Human Rights." He had, of course, no illusions that his constitution was
anything more than a working outline, an invitation to constructive
discussion of the fundamental issues confronting the nation.

LATE IN 1989, dismayed by Gorbachev's failure to move decisively on
constitutional and economic reforms, Sakharov—supported by Yuri
Afanasiev, Arkady Murashev, Gavriil Popov, and Vladimir Tikhonov—

---

*The Nationalities Factor in Soviet Politics and Society, Westview Press, 1990, p.
318.

called on the people of the country to stop work for two hours on December 11. He hoped that such a demonstration would persuade the second meeting of the Congress of People's Deputies, scheduled to open on December 12, to abolish the Constitution's Article 6, which ordained the Communist Party's monopoly of power,* and to enact new laws on property that would free the economy from bureaucratic dictates.

This appeal to workers and peasants for direct political action alarmed the authorities and disconcerted those members of the intelligentsia who feared the masses and any independent initiatives on their part. On December 12, the first day of the Congress, an irritated Gorbachev cut short Sakharov's arguments for speedy action on the reform agenda, and on December 14, the last day of Sakharov's life, a stormy caucus of the Interregional Group fretted about the strike call and debated whether deputies on the left ought to declare themselves a formal opposition. In reply, Sakharov addressed this plea to his wavering allies:

What is the meaning of political opposition? We simply cannot share responsibility for the actions of a government that is leading the nation to disaster and postponing the realization of *perestroika* for years to come. During that time the country will fall apart, collapse. All the plans to go over to a market economy have turned out to be impractical; despair is deepening and will bar the road to evolutionary development. The only way, the only chance, for peaceful reform of the system is a radical quickening of *perestroika*.

When we declare that we are going into opposition, we assume responsibility for the measures we propose—this is a second, extremely important implication of that term. There is a profound crisis of popular confidence in the Party and government which can be overcome only by decisive action. Repeal of Article 6 and related provisions of the Constitution would make a political statement transcending the immediate legal consequences of that step, and we

*Gorbachev's opposition prevented repeal of Article 6 in December 1989, but he rather quickly reversed his stance, and in March 1990 a special session of the Congress did away with it. During the same session, the Congress also amended the Constitution to provide for a President of the USSR. Gorbachev was chosen by the Congress to fill this post, but future Presidents will be elected by universal, equal, and direct suffrage for five-year terms.

need this statement today, not a year from now when work on a new constitution will have been completed. We have to restore momentum to *perestroika* without delay.

And we must restore faith in our Interregional Group—over the past several months, after awakening such high hopes, it has begun to lose credibility.

And finally, I would like to respond to the accusation that the call for a two-hour political strike was a gift to the right wing, and that the gift would be augmented by our declaration of opposition to the government. I categorically reject this notion. Our appeal initiated a country-wide discussion this past week which has greatly expanded political participation. It's not a question of how many workers actually stopped work, although there were quite a few strikes in the Donets coal fields, in Vorkuta, in Lvov, and elsewhere. What matters is that the people have finally found a means to express their will and are ready to support us politically. The events of the past week have proved this, and we dare not lose their support. For us to fail to take action now would be a *real* gift to the right wing; that is all they need from us in order to triumph.

This was Sakharov's last public address. He returned to his home and, after a hasty meal, retired to his study to prepare for "tomorrow's battle" in the Congress. Two hours later, his wife found him dead.

During the four days of national mourning that followed, tens of thousands of Soviet citizens from all walks of life paid tribute to the brave and brilliant man who had done so much to restore their faith in themselves and to repair the fatal breach between state and society. When asked to comment on Sakharov's death, Gorbachev responded: "He was not some sort of political intriguer, but a person with his own ideas and convictions, which he expressed openly and directly. I valued this in him, although I did not always agree with him." Some have disdained these words as feeble praise, but they were in truth an exceptional tribute to Sakharov from a leader surrounded by sycophants, ambitious office-seekers, and scheming rivals. Sakharov's scientific colleague Roald Sagdeyev grieved: "I don't know how we'll continue without his absolute integrity. . . . We have lost our moral compass." And Tatyana Zaslavskaya, a deputy, said: "Sakharov was the only one among us who made no compromises. That he suffered for all of us gave him an authority that no one else had. Without him, we could not begin to rebuild our society or ourselves."

The fact that the Soviet Union has come so far—and it has come unbelievably far in the past four years—is a tribute to Andrei Sakharov and to the credo he stated in his Nobel lecture and practiced throughout his public career: "We must make good the demands of reason and create a life worthy of ourselves and of the goals we only dimly perceive." Inspired by Sakharov's example, a whole crop of vigorous young deputies are at work in the national and local Soviets striving to establish responsible, democratic government in the USSR. It is a fragile experiment; time is needed, and the immediate difficulties that must be managed are prodigious. But there is good reason to believe that in the end reason and the human spirit will triumph, and a free people and a democratic government will become Andrei Sakharov's lasting monuments.

* * *

In *Moscow and Beyond,* for the benefit of readers not familiar with the *Memoirs,* persons and events introduced in the earlier volume have been identified in footnotes. I am responsible for these and all other footnotes and editorial interpolations. For the most part, the English text follows the Russian text, published in the United States by Chekhov Publishing Corporation, except for cuts of a few passages of little interest to the Western reader, and adjustments of order and tense where there was risk of confusion. Transliteration, as in the *Memoirs,* generally follows the Library of Congress system.

The author has included acknowledgments in his preface. I would like to express my own thanks to Melvin Rosenthal, whose conscientious copy-editing has significantly improved the English text, and to Andrew Blane for his assistance with this introduction.

September 30, 1990   Edward Kline

PREFACE

In December 1986, my wife Lusia and I were allowed to return to Moscow—after seven years of isolation in Gorky, our exile had come to an end.

My *Memoirs*, which I had basically completed by November 1983, together with Lusia's account of our years in exile,* tell the story of my life from childhood through December 1986. In Moscow in 1987 and in Newton and Westwood, Massachusetts, in 1989, I was able to edit my manuscript, and also to describe events from the time of our arrival back in Moscow through my participation in the June 1989 Congress of People's Deputies. Although I originally intended to include these additional chapters in *Memoirs*, they grew in length, and I decided to publish them as a separate book.

I would like to express my appreciation to Efrem Yankelevich, Edward Kline, Ashbel Green, Antonina Bouis, and everyone who worked on *Moscow and Beyond*. Lusia was its first editor.

Moscow
December 1989

Andrei Sakharov

*Published as *Alone Together*, by Elena Bonner (Alfred A. Knopf, 1986). Sakharov uses her childhood name, Lusia, when referring to his wife.

MOSCOW
AND BEYOND

1

BACK IN MOSCOW

ON THE MORNING of December 23, 1986, Lusia and I stepped off the train at Moscow's Yaroslavl Station onto a platform teeming with reporters from all over the world—and, as I learned later, from the Soviet Union as well. It took me forty minutes to make my way through the crowd. Lusia had been separated from me, hundreds of flashbulbs blinded me, and microphones were continually thrust into my face while I tried to respond to the barrage of questions. This impromptu media event was the prototype of many to follow: the whole scene offered a preview of the hurly-burly life that now awaited us.

I spoke of prisoners of conscience, naming many; of the need to pull Soviet troops out of Afghanistan; of my thoughts on the Strategic Defense Initiative (SDI) and Soviet insistence that American renunciation of SDI was a precondition for negotiations on nuclear weapons—the so-called "package principle"; of *perestroika* and *glasnost;* and of the contradictory and complex nature of these processes. For a while, I gave several interviews a day to newspapers, magazines, and television companies from all over the world, but fortunately the pace slackened a bit after January.

I especially remember an interview transmitted live by satellite from the studio in Ostankino—all the advanced space technology, the multiple screens with my strangely unfamiliar face against the blue sky, and the most intimidating part, the "black hole" of the camera. For this first "telebridge," the interpreter was Alex Goldfarb, who had translated at press conferences in our Chkalov Street apartment before he emigrated to New York. The very possibility of such broadcasts was astonishing—a sign of a new era, of *glasnost*.

Lusia and I were almost buried under the load of those first few months; but we had no choice, we had to carry on. What has life in Moscow been like since our return? I have to spend time preparing written responses (which Lusia types out) for almost all major interviews; I just can't do it any other way. People pass through the house endlessly—and we so want to be alone. Lusia cooks not just for two, as in Gorky, but for a whole crowd. Long after midnight, it's by no means uncommon to find Lusia, despite her heart attacks and her bypasses, mopping the landing—our building is self-service—and myself still at work on a statement to be issued the following day. Besides interviews, there are hundreds of things to do: another letter to Gorbachev, a foreword for Anatoly Marchenko's book,* preparations for the Forum. And people, people, people: friends, acquaintances, would-be acquaintances, refuseniks, foreigners in Moscow who feel duty-bound to meet Sakharov, European ambassadors, Western scientists—it's a constant madhouse.

Once the mass release of political prisoners began, Lusia kept a running list in order to report their names and any hitches that developed to the news agencies. The foreign correspondents (and the radio commentators) often made egregious errors, so that instead of Lusia's report on a hunger strike by the Ukrainian dissident Mykola Rudenko, who was demanding information on the fate of his confiscated archive, we would hear Western broadcasters saying that Academician Sakharov had announced a hunger strike by Rudenko demanding permission to emigrate, and that Sakharov's wife had asserted that this affair demonstrated the negative side of Kremlin policy—words she never could or would have said, since they're not her style, to put it mildly. There were comparable mistakes almost every day; even my statements on SDI came out garbled.

That was our everyday life. Perhaps I have delusions of grandeur, but I want to believe that this wasn't all wasted motion or a game. I don't mind if the process was inefficient so long as it actually promoted the release of political prisoners, the preservation of peace, and disarmament.

---

*To Live Like Everyone, Henry Holt, 1989. Marchenko, a prominent dissident, died on December 8, 1986, while on hunger strike in Chistopol Prison.

* * *

WHAT DID I SAY in my first interviews? I stressed over and over again
that the release of all prisoners of conscience would demonstrate the
depth, authenticity, and irreversibility of democratic change in our country, that the continuing detention of people who had spoken out too
soon for *glasnost* betrayed a lack of consistency in the current course.
I would then name up to a dozen prisoners whose cases I knew well.

In mid-January 1987, an interview given by a Soviet representative at
the Vienna Follow-Up Meeting to the Helsinki Accords and other
omens pointed to the early release of a substantial number of prisoners
of conscience. At the same time, recalling my conversations with Andreyev and Marchuk,* I worried that it might fall short of our dream
of a complete and unconditional amnesty. I decided to write another
letter to Gorbachev:

> Without an amnesty, it will be impossible to bring about a
> decisive moral change in our country, to overcome the inertia of
> fear, indifference, and hypocrisy. Not, of course, that an amnesty
> alone is sufficient for that. . . . I will be frank. This matter should
> not be simply turned over to the same agencies that in the past have
> committed or sanctioned illegal and unjust acts [the KGB, the
> Procurator's office, the courts, and the Ministry of Internal Affairs].
> . . . It would be a shame if an amnesty decree became simply a
> license to extort recantations and promises to abstain from "antiso-
> cial behavior" from prisoners, and an exoneration of the agencies
> I have mentioned. . . . I think it would be a good idea for the
> Central Committee to convene a meeting on the subject, possibly
> inviting representatives of the human rights movement and repre-
> sentatives of the cultural and scientific intelligentsia. [I proposed
> Sofia Kalistratova, Larisa Bogoraz, Mikhail Gefter, and Sergei Kova-
> lev as possible candidates.]

*In October 1986, Deputy Procurator General Vladimir Andreyev met with Sa-
kharov in Gorky to discuss his appeal for prisoners of conscience (see *Memoirs*, pp.
611–12). On December 19, three days after Gorbachev invited Sakharov to return to
Moscow, he sent Guri Marchuk, president of the Academy of Sciences, to Gorky to brief
Sakharov on the political situation and the current Soviet stand on disarmament (*Memoirs*, pp. 616–17).

I received no answer to this letter.

Meanwhile, the long-awaited release of political prisoners had begun. By April 1987 (when I first began writing this book) about 160 prisoners had been freed before the end of their terms. Is that a lot or a little? By comparison with earlier experience and with our most optimistic expectations, it was a lot—an extraordinarily great number. But at least twice as many prisoners of conscience remained in prisons, camps, exile, or psychiatric hospitals. By 1988, virtually all the well-known prisoners had been released. But there are still many persons (whose names we may not know) in psychiatric hospitals or serving time on dubious charges—I include in this category conscientious objectors, illegal border-crossers, victims of trumped-up criminal charges, and so on.

Moreover, it was not an *unconditional* release of prisoners of conscience, not an amnesty. Ex-convicts have not been rehabilitated, a measure that would confirm that their imprisonment had been unjust. Each case was reviewed individually, and each prisoner had to sign a statement that he would not in future indulge in "illegal" behavior. In effect, people had to "buy" their freedom, admitting by implication that they were guilty of crimes. (By "confessing" during their investigations or trials, many prisoners could have gained their freedom much sooner, but they refused to do so.) The fact that a prisoner could often satisfy this demand with some relatively innocuous banalities may have been important for the individual, but it didn't alter the situation in principle. And the officials responsible for unjust, illegal arrests and trials preserved the "honor of their uniform": the releases were formally recorded as pardons.

The procedure used provided no guarantee against a repetition of unlawful and arbitrary actions, and it degraded the moral and political significance of the government's truly bold step. Perhaps Gorbachev was forced to compromise with the KGB, whose support he still needs. But what if he was simply deceived? Or if he doesn't understand the importance of procedure? Much was left to local discretion, but that only begs the question. Still, it was probably the best we could hope for.

Back in 1987, Lusia, I, and Sofia Kalistratova, who shared our views, tried on several occasions to explain to political prisoners the options they faced and to make the choice easier for them. With all our hearts and souls we wished freedom and happiness for every prisoner of conscience; and, when all is said and done, the releases were significant and a move in the right direction, even if carried out in a mean-spirited fashion. But quite a few people disapproved of our behavior. Once, in early February, Larisa Bogoraz and Boris Altshuler* came to see us, and we had a difficult, painful discussion. We were forced to listen to accusations of having advocated shameful concessions, of having urged capitulations that could scar the prisoners for the rest of their lives. Kalistratova was the target of still sharper criticism. It was difficult to hear all this from people whom Lusia and I respect deeply, people who share many of our ideas and values; but disagreements are inevitable in dealing with difficult problems. I believe that they will pass—they have already begun to diminish.

AFTER A SEMINAR at FIAN† on December 30, 1986, I was approached by two journalists from *Literaturnaya gazeta:* Oleg Moroz, a reporter, and Yuri Rost, a photographer; they wanted to come to my apartment for an interview. After a few minutes' thought, I consented—on condition that I could see the final text and approve any cuts or corrections. They could either print my approved version without further change or kill the article. This would ensure that my views would not be distorted.

Moroz and Rost agreed, and on the spot handed me a sheet of paper with some preliminary questions. I was in a rush to get to the studio where I was to be interviewed via satellite, so I accepted their offer to drive me there. Talking with each other, they mentioned the name Yakovlev with approval, and then quickly turned to me, saying, "Don't worry, it's not the Yakovlev you slapped."‡ Moroz and Rost seemed in their off-hours like many other Moscow intellectuals I knew; in any event, they listened to Western radio regularly.

On January 1, 1987, while normal people were resting up after New Year's Eve celebrations, I was slaving over Moroz's not-so-simple ques-

---

*Bogoraz is a human-rights activist and the widow of Anatoly Marchenko. Altshuler, a theoretical physicist, and the son of one of Sakharov's colleagues on the H-bomb project, had earlier been fired from his academic post because of his activities on behalf of Sakharov.

†FIAN is the acronym for the Lebedev Physics Institute of the Academy of Sciences, where Sakharov was employed.

‡Sakharov slapped the historian Nikolai Yakovlev for viciously maligning his wife in the book *CIA Target—the USSR*. See *Memoirs*, pp. 585–92.

tions, while Lusia typed out and edited my answers. The questions—Afghanistan, prisoners of conscience, the package principle, nuclear testing—were the same ones foreign correspondents asked, and my answers had become almost standard, but I wanted my debut in the Soviet press to be as cogent as possible.

Moroz and Rost taped a first version of the interview on January 3, and submitted additional questions. During later sessions, they suggested a few acceptable changes and cuts and added three or four questions, which served to counter my more provocative answers. They told me that the interview had been approved by the managing editors, but not by Alexander Chakovsky, then editor-in-chief. It was making its way up the ladder, and had reached the "next-to-last" rung—this, they hinted, was Egor Ligachev [then a Senior Secretary of the Party's Central Committee with responsibility for ideological questions], with Gorbachev being the final rung. At our next meeting, however, they told me that publication had been shelved indefinitely, although they hoped the interview would be reconsidered after the January Plenum, which would "decide many things." In fact, it has never been published. *Glasnost* has not reached that stage. It's a shame; I hadn't pulled my punches in order to get it past the censors, and so its appearance in the Soviet press would have been a milestone for *perestroika.* *

Still, we profited from the interview even though it wasn't published. Lusia wrote in my name to Arkady Vaksberg, who reports on ethics and the legal system for *Literaturnaya gazeta*, about an arrest in Kiev, and I asked Rost and Moroz to deliver the letter. Pavel Protsenko, a librarian, had been charged with writing and keeping manuscripts on religious and historical subjects. A judge had remanded the case for further investigation, but Protsenko was held in custody pending trial. Vaksberg (without referring to me) reported this procedural violation to the procurator; Protsenko was released, and the case eventually was dropped.

ONE SUBJECT that comes up in every interview is my attitude toward Gorbachev and *perestroika*. Actually, it was important to work out an

---

*Although Moroz and Rost's 1986 interview was never printed, Rost published (in *Literaturnaya gazeta*, November 16, 1988) a profile of Sakharov incorporating some of the earlier material.

answer to this question for my own sake. While we were still in Gorky, we began to notice astonishing changes in the press, the movies, and television. Vaksberg's articles on the Supreme Court contained passages that a short while before would have led to his indictment for slandering the Soviet system. For example, he reported that 70 percent of the letters written to the procurator's office by persons seeking a reexamination of their cases and receiving the standard response—"No basis for review"—lacked any notation showing that the file had been pulled and checked; in other words, the response had been automatic and perfunctory. He wrote up the case of fourteen people who had confessed to a murder and had been tried, convicted, and executed, and who were later shown to have had no connection with the crime; the confessions must have been extracted by beatings or other torture.

Glasnost, thank goodness, is continually breaking new ground, and has made more headway in the press than anywhere else. But while frank and open public debate serves as the cutting edge of *perestroika*, action doesn't necessarily follow; the gap between word and deed has been growing. And some areas are still taboo: heretical opinions about international policies, criticism of leading Party figures (although government ministers are now fair game), most statistics, information about prisoners of conscience, and so on. I have been disturbed by the skimpy and one-sided coverage of the conflict between Azerbaijan and Armenia, as well as the reporting of certain other sensitive subjects. Unfortunately, *glasnost* seems to be spinning its wheels in just those cases where it might most benefit society. Another sign of trouble was the difficulty in ordering 1989 subscriptions for the more politically daring periodicals. This was apparently a temporary concession—since revoked—to opponents of *perestroika*.

Perestroika involves more than *glasnost*. Important social and economic changes are underway: greater autonomy for industrial and commercial enterprises; decentralization of management; a more substantive role for local soviets, which in the past have been overshadowed by Party bodies. The Central Committee Plenum held in June 1987 was devoted to economic reform and the proposal to free enterprises from detailed central planning and to grant them complete financial independence. Firm decisions resolving these vital questions, even if they have to be implemented gradually, could make a real difference. During the January 1987 Plenum, Gorbachev called for changes in promotion policy and in the selection of Party and government officials and industrial managers that would have a significant impact on our political system—if they are adopted. Plans for reform of the Criminal Code and other legislation were also discussed at that Plenum. And there was new thinking about international issues as well, but I will defer my comments on that subject.

Overall, however, examples of *perestroika* in practice—as distinct from rhetoric—are rare, and the few that do exist demonstrate its partial, tentative, and erratic character. I've mentioned my misgivings about the inconsistent and still incomplete release of prisoners of conscience. The Law on Individual Enterprise is timid and vague: it does not provide stimulants for entrepreneurial activity; it severely limits the number of persons eligible to participate; and it contains many other restrictions. Its thrust was further blunted by the practically simultaneous adoption of a law on "unearned" income that in effect allows criminal prosecution of individual entrepreneurs and was initially applied in ridiculous ways. As soon as the Law on Cooperatives was passed, the Ministry of Finance established a tax rate so high (up to 90 percent of income) that it virtually barred the development of cooperatives. The crucial Law on State Enterprise does not contain guarantees for enterprise autonomy in planning and financial matters, even with respect to the disposition of profits.

One aspect of *perestroika* that enjoys my whole-hearted support is the campaign against alcoholism; but here, too, experience has shown that things weren't thought through with sufficient care.

What is my overall appraisal? In 1985, while confined in Semashko Hospital, I watched one of Gorbachev's early television appearances, and I told my roommates (I had no one else to talk to): "It looks as if our country's lucky. We've got an intelligent leader." I repeated this opinion in December 1986 during my first interview by satellite, and my initial, positive reaction has remained basically unchanged. It seems to me that Gorbachev, like Khrushchev, is an extraordinary personality who has managed to break free of the limits customarily respected by Party officials. What, then, explains the inconsistencies and half-measures of the new course? The main stumbling block, as I see it, is the inertia of a gigantic system, the resistance, both passive and active, of innumerable bureaucratic and ideological windbags. Most of them will be out of a job if there is a real *perestroika*. Gorbachev has spoken of this bureaucratic resistance in some of his speeches, and it sounds like a cry for help.

But there's more to it than that. The old system, for all its drawbacks, worked. Changing over to a different system involves the problems of any transition: a lack of experience in working in the new way, a scarcity of managers of the new type. After all, people had grown accustomed to the old system, which at least guaranteed a minimal standard of living. Who knows what the new one will bring?

And lastly, Gorbachev and his close associates themselves may still not have completely thrown off the prejudices and dogmas of the system they inherited.

The restructuring of our country's command-type economic system is an extremely complex matter. Without the introduction of market relations and elements of competition, we are bound to see serious shortages, inflation, and other negative phenomena. In actual fact, our country is already in economic trouble; everywhere, food and other necessities are in short supply.

Another thing concerns me greatly—the zigzags on the road to democracy. It seems as if Gorbachev is trying to gain control of the political situation and strengthen his personal power by compromising with the forces opposed to *perestroika* instead of relying on democratic reforms. That's extremely dangerous. Only a nationwide surge of initiative can give substance to democracy, and our chiefs are not ready for this—as shown, for example, by the 1988 law placing unconstitutional restrictions on meetings and demonstrations.

The situation is incredibly snarled and riddled with contradictions. The progressive replacement of key personnel, the country's objective need for *perestroika,* and the fact that "the new always beats the old" (to quote Stalin's famous phrase that was drummed into our heads when I was young) should all work in Gorbachev's favor. He has four levers that he can use to move the country forward: *glasnost* (this is proceeding under its own steam); the new personnel policies; the new international policies aimed at slowing the arms race; and democratization.

It was along these lines that I spoke in all my 1987 interviews, with varying degrees of detail. I recall with particular satisfaction a telephone interview with Zora Safir Hopkins, a correspondent for the Voice of America; a detailed talk for Italian television about Gorbachev's speech at the January Plenum; and an interview with *Der Spiegel.* (I would like to take this opportunity to correct my statement in *Der Spiegel* that

Pyotr Kapitsa didn't defend me while I was in Gorky. I have since learned that he sent a telegram to Brezhnev and wrote a long letter on my behalf to Andropov.*)

My positive attitude toward *perestroika* is not accepted by everyone: it especially upset some dissidents in the USSR and émigrés in the West. One Russian-language newspaper in New York printed an article with the headline "The Pardoned Slave Helps His Master," or something of the sort. (The reference to Radzinsky's play was rather spoiled by the writer's confusion of Lunin and Lenin.) I was more upset by a critical article written by Malva Landa, a courageous, honest person, which accused me of uncritical collaboration with the authorities. It's sad, but what can I do? I hope that this disagreement too will pass, like the one with Bogoraz and Altshuler.

DURING THE FIRST MONTHS after our return from Gorky, most Western ambassadors paid calls, and we received them as we did our many other visitors, in our rather cramped apartment, now sorely in need of repairs after seven years of neglect. Lusia would serve them tea, coffee, and cake.

On February 5, 1987, a delegation organized by the U.S. Council on Foreign Relations came to see us. Henry Kissinger, Cyrus Vance, Harold Brown, William Hyland, Jeane Kirkpatrick, General David Jones, Michael Mandelbaum, Charles Mathias, Jr., Peter Peterson, and Peter Tarnoff were potent actors on the world scene; their visit was an expression of respect for me and for my international prestige. They posed questions, and I stated as clearly as I could my position on *perestroika*, on useful Western responses, on disarmament, on SDI, on human rights, and on *glasnost.*

I stressed the West's vital interest in having the USSR become an open, democratic society with a normal economic, social, and cultural life. Much of the discussion revolved around this issue, and Kissinger posed a blunt question: "Is there a danger that the USSR will first effect

*See Sakharov's *Memoirs*, Alfred A. Knopf, 1990, pp. 303–304, for excerpts from Kapitsa's appeals.

a democratic transformation, accelerating its scientific and technological progress and improving its economy, and then revert to expansionist policies and pose an even greater threat to peace?" I replied that the issue was a serious one, but what people should fear is not the normal development of an open, stable society and a powerful peacetime economy in the USSR, but rather the disruption of the world's equilibrium potentially posed by the military buildup of an internally closed and externally expansionist society. I have since argued, in answering similar questions, that the West should encourage the process of *perestroika*, cooperating with the USSR on disarmament and on economic, scientific, and cultural issues. But support should be given with "eyes wide open," not unconditionally. The opponents of *perestroika* should understand that their triumph, and a retreat from reform, would mean the immediate termination of Western assistance.

Harold Brown and Cyrus Vance asked my opinion of SDI. In response to my counter-question—would Congress sanction deployment of SDI if the USSR abandoned the package principle?—my guests assured me that a Soviet reversal on this issue would change the political situation and Congress would not fund a deployment of SDI in space. When I spoke about prisoners of conscience and emigration, Jeane Kirkpatrick paid particular attention and took notes; she struck me as an intelligent and tough-minded woman.

We didn't invite photographers or television reporters into the apartment, but we did allow them to take pictures of us on the street. It was reminiscent of our return to Moscow, with almost as many flashbulbs popping. Lusia made her "trademark" dessert, a cheese pastry, to accompany the coffee; Jeane Kirkpatrick praised it highly, and Henry Kissinger said it reminded him of the pastries his mother, Paula, used to bake when he was a child.

I HAD two lengthy conversations with the presidents of several American universities. They arrived in Moscow on January 24 and left on January 26 for Vienna, where they met with delegates to the Follow-Up Meeting on the Helsinki Accords. Herman Feshbach, a physicist from MIT, was traveling in their party, and we had a good talk on the evening of the 25th, primarily about SDI. Feshbach has been helpful to our children for many years. Lusia had met him in 1979 and again on her most recent visit, but until this meeting I had known him only by reputation and through his books on physics.

Alexei [Semyonov], Lusia's son, accompanied the college presidents to Moscow as an interpreter and, of course, to see us. He had left nine years earlier with little hope of ever returning, but he received a tourist visa just before the group's departure from New York, after I sent telegrams to the Soviet Embassy in Washington and to the ambassador, Yuri Dubinin. Alexei stayed on for six days after the rest of the party left, and so had an opportunity to tell us interesting details of American life. During a vacation from graduate school, he'd found odd jobs through an employment agency. He would show up at 6 A.M., and by 9, someone would hire him for the day to collect garbage, to substitute for an absent salesperson, to load trucks, to paint, or to do something else. Alexei was quickly marked down as a conscientious worker, and had no trouble finding jobs. He averaged $30 to $35 a day, not bad pay by Soviet standards. Alexei also told us about the use of referendums to decide controversial issues in city or state government, about health care, about education, and so on.

Toward the end of his stay, Alexei displayed symptoms of nervous exhaustion. The stress caused by our exile to Gorky has taken a toll on all the children. I finally learned some details of their long struggle, their travels around the world on our behalf, the anxiety caused by my hunger strikes, by the false report of my death in 1984, and by Lusia's open-heart surgery. All that time, Alexei was writing his dissertation, teaching, and working as a computer programmer.

Ed Kline, his wife, Jill, their daughter Carole, and Carole's friends Gwen and Richard arrived in time to celebrate Lusia's birthday on February 15. In my *Memoirs,* I have described Kline's role in publishing samizdat in the West, and his other human rights activities. Lusia met him in 1975, and had told me many times about his invaluable assistance to the children, but I had never expected that we would someday see each other in Moscow. I don't think either of us was disappointed. I was able to confirm for myself his advance notice as an intelligent, perceptive, and tactful person. I showed him the drafts for my talks at the Forum, and his approval was important to me.

2

THE MOSCOW FORUM

THE FORUM for a Nuclear-Free World and the Survival of Mankind opened in Moscow on February 14, 1987, and lasted for three days. This was a well-organized undertaking, staged primarily for propaganda purposes. Evgeny Velikhov, a vice-president of the Academy, was one of the directors of the Forum, and he invited me to take part.

I met Velikhov for the first time in early January. The Italian physicist Antonino Zichichi had come to Moscow with the idea of organizing a "World Laboratory," an international interdisciplinary research center that would work on ten to thirty scientific problems of great practical or theoretical significance. I am not the one to judge whether this is a useful project or primarily a matter of public relations and politics. It reminds me of Mikhail Lavrentiev's founding of the Siberian Division of the Academy of Sciences in 1957. There was a public relations element in that scheme too, but it seems to have been justified by results.

Zichichi wanted to include a Magnetic Thermonuclear Reactor (MTR) among the Laboratory's projects; this was the reason for my invitation to Velikhov's office, where Academician Boris Kadomtsev, a theoretical physicist working on MTRs, briefed us on recent advances in controlled fusion reactions and ongoing research—extremely interesting for me, as I hadn't followed developments since the 1960s. It turns out that a constant circular current can be produced in a torus by means of a high-frequency field; successful experiments have been conducted in Japan, although so far they have been limited to a low plasma density. Methods for the continuous introduction of thermonuclear fuel have also been worked out, eliminating a major drawback of tokamaks—their inability to function nonstop.*

Zichichi explained his projects and discussed them with Velikhov. I limited myself to asking questions, but as our conversation drew to a close, I invited Zichichi to visit me later at home.

After the meeting broke up, Velikhov drove me back to Chkalov Street, and brought up the Forum. I quickly let him know the dim view I took of the package principle. Velikhov said simply that he had a different opinion, and he invited me to attend private discussions on disarmament that he had organized with Academicians Roald Sagdeyev, Vitaly Goldansky, and Boris Raushenbakh.

That evening, Zichichi and his wife came for a visit, unexpectedly accompanied by Velikhov—he was apparently under orders not to leave us alone together. A lively conversation took place around the kitchen table. Velikhov, wanting to seem like a "regular fellow," uncorked a bottle of wine, and in general his manner was informal, almost as if he were in his own home. At the same time, he behaved with a certain tact—even, perhaps, a measure of respect. It was all a bit ironic, since Velikhov, like other Academy bigwigs, had told all sorts of fairytales about me while I was in Gorky, even during my hunger strikes. (In a conversation with one foreigner—Velikhov was evidently not aware of our friendly relations—he established some sort of record in this campaign, when he referred to information received from my first wife, who "lived in his building": Klava died in 1969, and Velikhov lives in a one-family house.)

A week later, the secretary of the Forum's organizing committee invited me to a meeting at the Space Research Institute chaired by Velikhov and Sagdeyev, then the Institute's director. Twenty or more people had gathered in a small room to hear Velikhov describe the Forum's program, and I asked questions which the others answered. I got the impression that the meeting had been convened on my account; certainly what I learned was helpful in preparing my speeches for the Forum and bolstering my confidence. Afterward, Sagdeyev invited me to watch a spectacular documentary film on Halley's Comet.

---

*See *Memoirs*, Chapter 9, for Sakharov's role in the development of MTRs. The tokamak system, which evolved from Sakharov's pioneering work, is perhaps the most promising approach to the thermonuclear generation of power.

After another week or two, and a second session of the organizing committee held at the presidium of the Academy, Velikhov asked me to stay on "because Guri Ivanovich [Marchuk] wants to talk to you." We waited for forty minutes in Velikhov's office, which was decorated with cartoons, apparently mementos of some celebration; his shelves were filled with reference books and souvenirs. Velikhov talked about his work on the State Committee for the Utilization of Atomic Energy and about the difficulties and foolishness caused by the absence of rational regulatory mechanisms in the economy.

Finally, a secretary called to announce Marchuk's arrival, and we went to his office. Velikhov briefed him on the Forum. Marchuk asked whether I intended to speak, and, if so, what would be the gist of my remarks. He added, as he had in our December talk, that I enjoyed great international prestige, and that my support for the USSR's peace initiatives was important. He let it be understood, if not in these exact words, that he was talking on behalf of "Mikhail Sergeyevich [Gorbachev], who is having a difficult time." I said that I did intend to speak, and very briefly outlined my ideas, stressing that an agreement on the reduction of strategic nuclear missiles should not be linked to agreement on SDI. Velikhov objected vigorously to my rejection of the package principle, and he was backed by Marchuk. I said I was convinced that I was right and that my participation in the Forum made sense only because my ideas on peace and disarmament differed from the official line. Our discussion educated me on the case for the package principle and sharpened my own arguments against it.

A week before the Forum it occurred to me (rather belatedly) to invite Efrem Yankelevich [Elena Bonner's son-in-law and Sakharov's representative in the West] to Moscow to assist me and to act as interpreter for my conversations with foreign scientists, but he didn't receive a visa at that time.

Before the Forum opened, a delegation from the Federation of American Scientists, headed by Jeremy Stone and Frank von Hippel, came to see us. They explained the Federation's positions, and von Hippel showed me an outline of his report to the Forum.

For two days (February 14 and 15), the participants in the Forum were divided into sections (science, business, religion, culture, politics, etc.). On the third and last day, everyone assembled at the Kremlin for a speech by Gorbachev and a banquet. The science section, which met at the Cosmos Hotel, was headed by von Hippel, but it was really Velikhov who called the shots. I was the main draw for many Western participants, and was constantly "attacked" during and after the sessions, in the hallways of the Cosmos and at home. I made up a little ditty that began: "The Forum has closed up shop,/ But at our door the knocking doesn't stop." Nevertheless, the ordeal was worth it; after many years of isolation, this was my first public appearance, and my first opportunity to present my views before a large audience.

THERE WERE four sessions of the scientific section: reducing strategic nuclear arsenals; European security; anti-missile defenses; and the banning of underground nuclear tests. I spoke at the first, third, and fourth sessions. During my initial talk, I touched on general issues:

As a citizen of the USSR, I direct my appeals to the leadership of our country in particular, along with the other great powers with their special responsibility for the world situation.

International security and real disarmament are impossible without greater trust between the nations of the West and the USSR and other socialist countries. There must be a settlement of regional conflicts on the basis of compromise and restoration of stability wherever it has been disrupted. Support for destabilizing and extremist forces and all terrorist groups should be ended, along with attempts to expand the sphere of influence of one side at the expense of the other. All countries should work together on economic, social and ecological problems. Greater openness and democracy in our country are necessary. We need the free flow of information; the unconditional and complete release of prisoners of conscience; the freedom to travel and to choose one's country and place of residence; effective control by the people over the formulation of domestic and foreign policy.

Despite the continuing process of democratization and the increasing openness in the country, the situation remains contradictory and unsettled, and some instances of backward movement can be observed (for example, the new decree on emigration). Without a resolution of political and humanitarian problems, progress in disarmament and international security will be extremely difficult if not impossible.

Conversely, democratization and liberalization in the USSR—and the economic and social progress closely associated with them—will be impeded unless the arms race slows down. Gorbachev and his supporters, who are waging a difficult struggle against ossified, dogmatic and self-seeking forces, have an interest in disarmament, in making sure that huge material and intellectual resources are not diverted to producing new and more sophisticated weapons.

But the West and the entire world also have an interest in the success of reforms in the USSR. An economically strong, democratic, and open Soviet Union will be a very important guarantor of international stability, a good and reliable partner in the common resolution of global problems. On the other hand, if the West tries to use the arms race to exhaust the USSR, the future will be extremely gloomy. A cornered opponent is always dangerous. There is no chance that the arms race can exhaust Soviet material and intellectual resources and that the USSR will collapse politically and economically; all historical experience indicates the opposite. But the process of democratization and liberalization will stop. The scientific and technical revolution will assume a pronounced military-industrial character, and as one might fear, expansionist tendencies and alliance with destructive forces will prevail in foreign policy.

The second part of my speech dealt with specific issues involved in the reduction of strategic weapons. Supporting in principle a simultaneous 50 percent cut in Soviet and American strategic weapons, I went on to say:

The "proportional" scheme is the simplest, and it is quite natural that progress should begin with that. But it is not the optimal outcome, since it does not address the problem of strategic stability.

A large part of the USSR's thermonuclear capability is in powerful, silo-based missiles with multiple warheads. Such missiles are vulnerable to a preemptive strike by the modern, highly accurate missiles of the potential enemy. It is of decisive importance here that a single enemy missile with multiple warheads can destroy several silo-based missiles. Given the rough equality of the U.S. and the USSR, one side would require only a portion of its own missiles to destroy all of the other side's silo-based missiles. In that situation, the strategic importance of being first to strike grows enormously. A country relying mainly on silo-based weapons may be forced in a critical situation to launch a first strike. This is an objective strategic reality that cannot be ignored by the opposing side.

I want to stress that no one planned this situation when silo-based missiles were deployed in the 1960s and 1970s. It arose as a result of the development and deployment of multiple warheads and the increase in missile accuracy. But today silo-based missiles—and, more generally, any missiles with vulnerable launch sites—constitute the principal source of military strategic instability.

For this reason I believe it is extremely important to give priority to cutting back missiles with vulnerable launch sites, i.e., missiles that are mainly first-strike weapons. That means first and foremost reducing the number of Soviet silo-based missiles, which are the backbone of Soviet thermonuclear forces, as well as U.S. MX missiles. Perhaps simultaneously with an overall reduction in numbers, some of the remaining Soviet silo-based missiles should be replaced by less vulnerable missiles with equivalent striking power (missiles using mobile or camouflaged launchers, cruise missiles with various basing modes, submarine-based missiles, and so on). I believe there is no need to replace U.S. MX missiles, since they play a smaller role in the overall balance and can simply be eliminated in the process of bilateral cuts.

The last issue I discussed in my first talk was the maximum reduction of strategic forces compatible with strategic stability. I explained the difficulty of arriving at a definitive answer, stressing that there is no precedent to help us decide a closely related issue, the limit of "acceptable" damage. This can't be calculated on the basis of a peacetime psychology, since in a bitterly contested war the level of "acceptable" loss might approach that level we usually associate with mutual assured destruction. I went on to say that:

In any event, this question can be postponed until after a 50 percent reduction has been implemented. A nuclear-free world is a desirable goal, but it will become possible only as the result of many radical changes in the world. The conditions for peaceful development, now and in the future, are settlement of regional conflicts; parity in conventional arms; liberalization, democratization, and greater openness of Soviet society; observance of civil and political rights; a compromise solution on the issue of antimissile defenses, without combining it in a package with other questions of strategic weapons.

I concluded on a positive note: "Convergence—a rapprochement of the socialist and capitalist systems—offers a real and lasting solution to the problem of international security." There was prolonged applause, as there had been for several other speakers. I was told that Anatoly Dobrynin, the former ambassador to the U.S. and at the time of the Forum chief of the Central Committee's International Department, was in the audience and left the hall immediately after my talk. (I can't remember now whether this happened on the 14th or the 15th.)

THE NEXT DAY I spoke about SDI. I noted the deadlock that had developed in disarmament negotiations, and then continued:

A significant cut in ICBMs and medium-range and battlefield missiles, and other agreements on disarmament, should be negotiated as soon as possible, independently of SDI, in accordance with the lines of understanding laid out in Reykjavik. I believe that a compromise on SDI can be reached later. In this way the dangerous deadlock in the negotiations could be overcome. I shall try to analyze the ideas that led to the package approach and demonstrate their unsoundness. I shall also attempt to demonstrate the unsoundness of the arguments in favor of SDI itself. I'll begin with the latter.

I'm convinced that the SDI system is not effective for the purpose for which its proponents claim it was intended. Antiballistic-missile (ABM) components deployed in space can be put out of action even in the nonnuclear stage of a war, and especially in the moment of transition to the nuclear stage, through the use of antisatellite weapons, space mines, or other means. Many key land-based ABM installations will also be destroyed. The use of ballistic missiles with lighter warheads and solid-fuel missiles with decreased boost-phase time will require an excessive increase in the number of SDI space stations.

ABM systems are of little use against cruise missiles and missiles launched from close range. Any ABM system, including SDI, can be effectively overcome by simply increasing the number of decoys and operational warheads, by jamming and by various methods of deception. All this as well as other considerations makes SDI a "Maginot line in space"—expensive and ineffective. Opponents of SDI maintain that even though it would be ineffective as a defensive weapon, it could create a shield behind which a first strike would be launched, since it might be able to repel a weakened retaliatory strike.

I think they are wrong. First, a retaliatory strike would not necessarily be greatly weakened. Second, almost all the arguments cited above regarding SDI's flaws in defending against a first strike would apply to a retaliatory strike as well.

Nevertheless, neither side seems prepared to abandon SDI research at this time, since the possibility of unexpected successes cannot be ruled out. What may be even more important and realistic is that the concentration of resources on the cutting edge of technology may result in important spinoffs in peaceful and military fields, such as in computer science. I still believe all these considerations and possibilities to be secondary in comparison with the enormous cost of SDI and the negative influence of SDI on strategic stability and disarmament negotiations.

Possibly SDI proponents in the U.S. are counting on an accelerated arms race, associated with SDI, to exhaust and ruin the economy of the USSR. This policy will not work and is extremely dangerous to international stability. In the case of SDI, an "asymmetric" response (i.e., a push to develop offensive forces and weapons to knock out an SDI system) would most efficiently frustrate such hopes. The claim that the existence of the SDI program has spurred the USSR to disarmament negotiations is also wrong. On the contrary, the SDI program is impeding those negotiations.

I would like to emphasize that attacks on space-based elements of hostile ABM systems during a nonnuclear stage of a major war could provoke escalation to a global thermonuclear war, in other words, to the destruction of the human race.

Everything I had to say in opposition to SDI, both at the Forum and before it, was widely quoted. The Soviet media, the press of some socialist countries, and Communist and left-wing publications in the West mentioned only that portion of my remarks. (Of course, any mention of me at all in the Soviet press, and what's more, in a respectful tone, was unusual at that time.) But my position on the package principle was also substantive, and much more important politically. Coverage on this issue was less detailed and often flawed; I was forced to issue several clarifications and corrections.

I opposed the package principle because I was convinced that an SDI defense could not be developed that would effectively block a retaliatory strike (let alone a first strike), and that, in any event, an asymmetrical response *would* prove feasible. Nevertheless, I accepted the premise that neither side would completely abandon research in a field that shows promise, however uncertain. I further surmised that the USSR's waiver of the package principle would create a new political and strategic climate in which the U.S. would not deploy antimissile defenses in space. (To the best of my knowledge, Reagan agreed in Reykjavik to a moratorium on SDI deployment.) On the other hand, if the USSR renounced the package principle and the U.S. nonetheless deployed SDI, we would simply revert to the current situation, with appreciable political gains for the USSR. The dismantling of missiles would be halted, and the USSR would deploy new, powerful missiles with invulnerable launchers as well as weapons that could destroy and eliminate SDI. I doubted that this scenario would appeal to the U.S.

Two weeks after the Forum, the USSR renounced the package principle for intermediate range missiles, and soon thereafter proposed the elimination of shorter-range missiles. This represented significant progress, but I continued to press for abandonment of the package with respect to ICBMs as well.*

---

*In September 1989, Foreign Minister Shevardnadze announced in Washington that disagreements on SDI need no longer bar an agreement on strategic nuclear weapons, and Gorbachev reiterated this shift in position at the December 1989 Malta summit.

Immediately after my morning speech on February 15, Jeremy Stone spoke for the Federation of American Scientists. He too called for renunciation of the package principle. Then Andrei Kokoshin, deputy director of Arbatov's Institute of the U.S.A. and Canada [an influential Soviet think-tank], contested my thesis that silo-based missiles pose a particular danger, saying that submarines aren't an ideal basing mode, either; they, too, aren't completely invulnerable. (This may be true, but it doesn't change the fact that silo-based missiles are first-strike weapons.) Then, to counter my criticism of the package, Velikhov said that scientists should not interfere in politics. But what, after all, was the Forum about? I'd been admonished not to meddle in politics by Marshal Nedelin, by Khrushchev, by Slavsky—every time I took some important and correct step. I think that my Forum speeches were appropriate forays into politics.

THE AFTERNOON of the 15th, I spoke again—this time on underground nuclear testing, a secondary issue with no real significance for arms control. I also discussed the peaceful use of atomic energy:

Nuclear weapons divide and threaten mankind. But there are peaceful uses of nuclear energy that should promote the unity of mankind. Speakers at the Forum have mentioned the disaster at Chernobyl, an example of the tragic interaction of equipment failure and human error. Nevertheless, the aversion that people rightly feel for military applications must not spill over to the peaceful use of nuclear energy. Mankind cannot do without nuclear power. We must find a solution to the safety problem that will rule out the possibility of another Chernobyl resulting from human error, failure to follow instructions, design defects, or technical malfunctions.

I then outlined my suggestion for the underground siting of nuclear reactors, and urged in conclusion "that people concerned about the potential harmful consequences of the peaceful use of nuclear energy should concentrate their efforts not on attempts to ban nuclear power, but instead on demands to assure its complete safety."*

While preparing for the Forum, I had wondered about the advisability of including these comments on the safe use of nuclear energy. Lusia convinced me I should do it; and of course she was right. She also wanted me to mention the need for a binding international agreement mandating the underground siting of future nuclear reactors and the progressive shutdown of existing aboveground reactors. I foolishly refrained from proposing this idea at the Forum, but I now call for such an international treaty at every opportunity.

A SPECIAL press conference, with me as the main attraction, was to take place at the press center of the Ministry of Foreign Affairs immediately after the sessions ended on the 15th. I made it a condition for my participation that Lusia and Ed Kline, my guest from the U.S., be present. The staff person in charge at first said that this would cause no problem, but late that afternoon he came over, red-faced, and explained that no one could attend except Forum participants. After a few moments' thought, I decided to yield on this point, since the alternative would have been a press conference in our apartment, inconveniencing everyone. I was taken to a large room where the other participants were waiting—von Hippel, Jerome Wiesner, Kokoshin, moderator Vladimir Pozner, and almost a hundred Western correspondents, many armed with cameras and microphones. Every seat was occupied, and people were standing or sitting on the floor. Von Hippel and Wiesner gave brief accounts of the science sessions, I then summarized my own remarks, and Kokoshin repeated his objections of that morning. Several questions were asked. It was over in an hour, and I hurried home, where guests were waiting to toast Lusia: for the first time in eight years, we would celebrate her birthday in Moscow together.

The final session of the Forum took place on the 16th, in the Kremlin Palace of Congresses. The section chairmen delivered reports, and then Gorbachev addressed the assembly. Von Hippel mentioned me in the

*For the full text of Sakharov's speeches at the Forum, see *Time*, March 16, 1987.

course of his talk—the article printed in *Izvestia* included his remarks, but omitted his reference to my Nobel Peace Prize.*

Several cameras, including Soviet ones, focused on me as I applauded passages of Gorbachev's speech [in which he called for the abolition of nuclear weapons by the year 2000 and a humanistic approach to international relations], and Lusia, who was watching at home, saw me on television.

After Gorbachev concluded, there was a great banquet. We received place cards—my seat was at the back of the hall with a group of physicians. We helped ourselves from buffet tables set with food and drink, including Georgian wine, despite the anti-alcohol campaign. I learned later from von Hippel that while I was busy talking to foreign and Soviet fans, who didn't leave me in peace for a second, Gorbachev had been sitting at the other end of the room with senior government officials. (Von Hippel had been placed at Gorbachev's table, and Mrs. Stone sat next to Raisa Gorbachev.) If I had known at the time, I would have tried to make my way to him in order to say a few words about prisoners of conscience and the package principle. More important, our encounter would have had political significance, and its absence was seen as a minor victory for the anti-Gorbachev forces.

Two incidents should have alerted me to the situation, but I caught on to their significance only after the fact. While waiting for the affair to begin, I had spoken with many people, including the writer Daniil Granin. Someone, apparently an aide from Intourist (or the Ministry of Foreign Affairs, or the KGB), brought over an elderly foreigner, announcing, "Andrei Dmitrievich, Mr. Hammer would like to speak with you."

I of course knew the name of one of the world's richest and most successful businessmen, who has maintained close and profitable ties with our country for more than sixty years and who has taken part in many humanitarian, philanthropic, and cultural affairs. Armand Hammer has met every Soviet leader from Lenin to Gorbachev. A trim man of medium build, he seemed tired and remote when our conversation began. In correct Russian, he pronounced a series of short sentences: "I think it is very important for a summit to take place this year. I will speak

---

*For von Hippel's speech, see *Bulletin of the Atomic Scientists*, May 1987.

about this with Gorbachev. I have some ideas about ending the war in Afghanistan. I will also speak about this with my friend General Zia, the President of Pakistan."

I said, "I think a good basis for a meeting between Gorbachev and Reagan would be the Soviet Union's renunciation of the package principle," and then gave a brief account of my remarks at the Forum.

Hammer grew interested, his face became animated, and a bright, concentrated sparkle came into his eyes. Our conversation was interrupted, however, by the famous ballerina Maya Plisetskaya, who led him away. The thought occurred to me that Hammer could pass on to Gorbachev the list of nineteen prisoners in the special-regimen camp whose fate particularly worried us. Just before the banquet began, I spotted the aide who had introduced me to Hammer (this time he had the actor Peter Ustinov in tow), and I asked him to escort me to Hammer. "I'll ask him to come to you." "That wouldn't be polite, I'll go to him. Please find him for me." He replied vaguely, and then Hammer did in fact come over, and I gave him the list for Gorbachev. Hammer, however, didn't seem very interested in the subject of prisoners.

I should have guessed then that Hammer was seated near Gorbachev and their table was off limits for me. Later, when I wanted to go to the toilet and walked toward that end of the room, two burly men in well-cut suits stopped me. "You can't go that way. Use the facilities at the other end." I still didn't realize that Gorbachev was close by, but even if I had, I don't know whether the security men would have let me through. (Bodyguards, after all, are serious people.)

AFTER THE FORUM, life remained hectic. Of the many meetings I had, I recall one with Daniel Ellsberg, the American who gained notoriety for leaking the Pentagon Papers to the press; he struck me as sincere, intelligent, erudite, passionate, and perhaps a bit inclined to go off the deep end. Our conversation was serious and interesting for me: we found that our views differed sharply, but not as much as one might expect considering his reputation as a "leftist." I also spoke with German "Greens"—Petra Kelly and Gert Bastian, a retired general.

In March, Margaret Thatcher invited Lusia and me to a luncheon at the British Embassy. Ambassador Bryan Cartledge and his wife, the

Foreign Minister Geoffrey Howe, and a translator were also at our table. I spoke, as usual, about prisoners of conscience, a subject that interested Howe, and about disarmament, calling attention to the opportunities offered by the USSR's willingness to uncouple elimination of medium-range missiles from the question of SDI. I stressed once again the importance of the West's supporting *perestroika* while simultaneously maintaining a firm line on human rights. In the course of our conversation, Howe recalled an exchange with Gromyko on the "Sakharov problem," probably in 1985. Gromyko had tried to turn it into a joke: "You know, I don't like sugar [*sakhar* in Russian] and never use it." The joke obviously jarred on Howe, and he still recalled it with marked perplexity.

In May, French Prime Minister Jacques Chirac paid an official visit to Moscow and attended a reception at the Academy of Sciences. He chatted alone with Marchuk for some twenty minutes and then addressed a select audience of Academicians. It was a fine speech, but I'm afraid many in the hall didn't understand it, since there was no translation (I was given the Russian text). In the interval between his session with Marchuk and his talk, Chirac spoke with me for ten minutes. We were surrounded by reporters, and every word was reported in the press. Chirac recalled, with many compliments, his meeting with Lusia in Paris, and I passed along her warm regards. I spoke about the special-regimen camp and about the failure to release many prisoners convicted of slandering the Soviet system. I brought up the Evsyukovs, who had been trying for many years to emigrate to France.* Later, with French correspondents, I spoke about Afghanistan, and mentioned Soviet bombing of hospitals organized there by volunteer physicians from France and Germany.

In early April I sent a letter to Foreign Minister Eduard Shevardnadze asking him to intercede on behalf of Merab Kostava,† a fellow Georgian. In May I received a phone call from an official named Ivanov of the Ministry of Foreign Affairs, who said, "You sent a letter to Minister Shevardnadze about the prisoner Kostava. I've been asked to inform you that he's been pardoned and is at liberty." Ivanov refused to tell me

---

*The Evsyukov family, who had experienced many trials and tribulations, were permitted to emigrate after Chirac's visit.

†Kostava, a musicologist and Georgian nationalist, was killed in an automobile crash in 1989.

whether my letter had any direct connection with Kostava's release, but I think his call speaks for itself.

An international seminar on quantum gravitation convened in Moscow in May. I saw John Wheeler for the first time since our memorable 1968 encounter in Tbilisi, and was introduced to the American physicist Stanley Deser. Their visit to our home was especially warm, thanks to Lusia; and, of course, to our remarkable guests. We spoke about public issues, SDI in particular, and about science. Wheeler was deeply interested in the foundations of quantum mechanics, and generally in the philosophical and epistemological questions that have been thrust into the spotlight by the revolutionary development of physics and cosmology in the twentieth century. I didn't understand everything he said, and I didn't always agree with him, but I was impressed by his scientific brilliance and powerful personality. Wheeler was collecting books and articles on the interpretation of quantum mechanics, but hadn't heard of Leonid Mandelshtam's lectures on indirect measurement; Evgeny Feinberg sent them to him at my request.*

I also met Stephen Hawking, known for his work on black holes and the radiation associated with them known as "Hawking radiation." I had earlier heard of his efforts on my behalf; now, our brief encounter and exchange of scientific clichés somehow led to a profound empathy between us.

I don't know the precise nature of Hawking's illness, but I could see its horrible effects—the muscular atrophy that restricts him to a wheelchair and has deprived him of speech.† He communicates through a special computer system. Words are displayed on a monitor, and with a barely perceptible movement of his fingers he can select the appropriate ones to create a sentence on the screen, A vocal synthesizer then pronounces the sentence aloud—with an American accent, Hawking complains, since the machine was made in the U.S. This contraption allows him to take part in scientific discussions, to write many papers containing deep and original ideas, and to communicate with his wife,

---

*Mandelshtam, an Academician, and mentor of Sakharov's teacher Igor Tamm, died in 1944. Feinberg was Sakharov's colleague at FIAN.

†Hawking suffers from amyotrophic lateral sclerosis (Lou Gehrig's Disease), a progressive deterioration of the central nervous system. He is the author of the best seller *A Brief History of Time*, Bantam, New York, 1988.

his children, and his friends. His morale is amazing: he has retained his good nature, his sense of humor, and his thirst for knowledge. His schedule keeps him on the go, traveling all over the globe and participating in many scientific seminars.

I saw Hawking several times, and once was present at a seminar where he "spoke" with a dozen scientists about the underlying principles of quantum mechanics and the "wave function of the universe" discussed in a paper he published, together with James Hartle, in 1984. During the seminar he wittily turned Einstein's celebrated epigram upside down, saying "God not only plays dice, but He throws them so far that they're beyond our reach."

After our first conversation, Hawking had given me reprints of several of his recent papers, including one on the direction of the arrow of time. I was glad that he had accepted the criticism of his colleague Don Page, concerning the erroneous assumption that the arrow reverses at the moment of maximum expansion of the universe and *maximum* entropy. I mentioned to Hawking that reversal is possible only under conditions of *minimum* entropy (but was too shy to bring up the simplest example, a closed universe in a state of false vacuum with positive energy and zero entropy). Hawking moved his fingers and the computer uttered its mechanical "yes" to signify his agreement. I regret my failure to tell him that I had first mentioned the idea of the reversal of the arrow of time in a state of minimum entropy in 1966 [see *Memoirs*, pp. 544–45] and had returned more than once to that theme.

A man I didn't know was hovering nearby while I was talking to Hawking. He later introduced himself, saying, "I'm Page." He opened an English-language Bible to a marked passage in the Gospel according to Matthew, and apparently wished to give me the book as a present. But I was embarrassed and didn't accept it—I don't read English that fluently, and besides, we have a Russian-language Bible, which we know well. . . .

Hawking's face and eyes haunted me for a long time.

IN LATE JUNE, I received diplomas from the French Academy of Sciences and the Academy of Moral and Political Sciences and the medal of the Institute of France. French scientists had been trying to arrange a presentation ceremony for many years, but it had to be delayed until our return to Moscow. Even then, the French were led down the garden path. During his visit to the USSR, Chirac asked Marchuk to organize something in France; or, if that proved difficult, in Moscow. Marchuk of course chose the latter. The Academy's foreign-relations administration gave its approval for a ceremony at the French Embassy at which diplomas and medals would be presented to me and to Vladimir Arnold, the son of my old mathematics professor, Igor Arnold, and himself a remarkably talented mathematician. He too had been elected to the French Academy of Sciences. Marchuk and Chirac also agreed that FIAN would organize an international seminar in our honor, but this wasn't put in writing.

Soviet scientists who were members of the French Academy of Sciences were invited to the ceremony. At the last moment, Marchuk informed the French Embassy that there would be no seminar, since it would create an "undesirable precedent." Two French physicists, Dr. Louis Michel and Dr. André Martin, protested this action on the part of the Academy—plainly dictated by outside forces—and refused to attend the ceremony. Other French scientists decided to go ahead with the long-postponed event despite the cancellation of the seminar. The delegation included the famous mathematicians Henri Cartan (with his wife) and Laurent Schwartz.

On June 29, 1987, I finally received my diplomas and medal, and then Arnold and I each said a few words. I repeated my ideas on the responsibilities of the scientist in the modern world—helping to preserve the peace; assuring essential human progress while making certain that scientific advances are applied in a safe manner; furthering trust and openness in society; and defending victims of injustice. Speaking about safety and progress, I mentioned the idea of siting nuclear reactors underground and again called for appropriate international legislation to regulate their construction.

I thanked everyone who had supported us during our Gorky exile, mentioning specifically the trip to Moscow of Dr. Michel and Dr. Pecker during our 1981 hunger strike. I deplored the failure of the Soviet Academy to speak out against my exile, and expressed the hope that the four members of the Academy, including Georgy Skriabin, its chief scientific secretary, who had signed an article slandering me, would one day disavow it. I also criticized the Academy's refusal to hold a seminar in conjunction with the award ceremony.

Very likely, the KGB was behind that veto: too many honors for me. Before the ceremony, we saw a KGB man standing near our car; later, we discovered that a windshield wiper had been stolen. That evening, after the ceremony, "persons unknown" smashed the car's rear window. The KGB was letting me know my bounds and was "defending" the Academy and Skriabin.

A FEW DAYS EARLIER, there had been a more unpleasant and vicious reminder of the ambivalence of our situation. A certain Roald Mukhamedyarov, who spent many years in camps and mental institutions and allegedly played some sort of games with the KGB, phoned and told me: "I'd prefer to meet with you in person, but I understand you're busy and your wife told me yesterday that it was OK to talk openly on the phone. I've been in touch with the KGB, including some of its top officers, but I won't mention any names. They told me that in late 1981 or early 1982 [he wasn't sure of the date], there was a plan to liquidate [murder] Elena Georgievna, but the decision was not approved at the highest level [apparently, he meant the Politburo]."

I told him that if Elena Georgievna were killed, I would kill myself. I asked for his source, and he said it was someone in the KGB, a general, but I have forgotten the department Mukhamedyarov mentioned, possibly one dealing with culture.

This call was almost certainly inspired by the KGB as a reminder and a threat. Nothing has happened so far, but you never can be sure. It's at least conceivable that murdering Lusia had been discussed at some level of the KGB. Perhaps they'd begun to believe their own lies and Yakovlev's scenario: an imperious, vain, and self-serving woman manipulating a meek old man in an ivory tower, once a scientific genius, now senile.

We've had sufficient evidence of the KGB's hatred of Lusia. Once, when I was in the hospital in Gorky, she went to buy bread and other groceries. As she got out of the car, she slipped in the mud and fell, bruising herself badly. (In fact, she had fractured her coccyx.) Lusia lay on the ground for several minutes, unable to get up. The KGB men who jumped out of the two surveillance cars laughed and jeered at her, and not one of them made a move to help her.

Murdering Lusia might have seemed like a solution for the "Sakharov problem," but apparently direct action—if it was ever discussed—was ruled out. Nonetheless, the persistent harassment I have described in my *Memoirs* could be construed as an attempt to eliminate Lusia without resorting to outright murder. After her heart attack, they may have hoped that nature would take its course, especially if they could keep doctors from treating Lusia, and could prevent her from traveling abroad—the tactics adopted. The scurrilous articles written by Nikolai Yakovlev were attempts to murder Lusia morally. Unfortunately, their assertions often fell on fertile soil. People are always looking for flaws in public personalities—"I come out on the stage . . . The darkness of the night is aimed at me along the sights of a thousand opera glasses."* Many people thought Lusia was the instigator of my hunger strikes; others expected her to remain abroad rather than return to her husband and to exile.

And even now, those who disapprove of something I have done—my defense of prisoners of conscience, my participation in the Forum, my attitude toward Gorbachev or *perestroika*, my criticism of SDI or of the package principle—tend to blame Lusia.

Just yesterday [written in July 1987], a refusenik, convinced of Lusia's total power over me, urged her to temper my criticism of SDI, so as not to alienate my supporters. According to him, my former friends are saying that "Sakharov isn't Sakharov anymore." Actually, Lusia's influence on me is enormous but not unlimited, and it operates on another plane than SDI, disarmament, and similar issues—it primarily affects questions involving human relations. It is based not on duress, but on our mutual love and our happy life together.

IN LATE MAY 1987, I was visited by Crimean Tatars who told me that for nearly a month their compatriot Bekir Umerov had been on a hunger strike to reinforce his request that Gorbachev receive a delegation of Crimean Tatars. I sent a telegram to Gorbachev about the Tatars, and another one to Umerov, asking him to end his fast: he did so after receiving my appeal. On July 7, I was visited by Reznikov, an official of

---

*From Boris Pasternak's poem "Hamlet," included in *Doctor Zhivago* (Harvill Press, 1958).

the Zhdanov District Party Committee, who brought a message for me: "A few days ago a delegation of Crimean Tatars was received by Comrade Pyotr Demichev, who assured them that the Soviet government would reexamine the question of autonomy." My hope at the time (as yet unfulfilled) was that this signaled a turning point for the Crimean Tatars.

FROM FEBRUARY to May 1987, Lusia (and I, to a lesser extent) had to spend a great deal of time and energy moving our possessions—literally thousands of books, journals, reprints, and letters—from Gorky to our Moscow apartments. Through the intervention of the Academy (which was clearly responding to orders), I had finally been given my own apartment in the Chkalov Street building, just one floor below Ruth's.* If only we'd enjoyed such luxury a dozen years ago! But, as the poet Alexander Mezhirov wrote: "Everything comes too late."

On June 6, Lusia's daughter, Tanya Yankelevich, escorted Ruth back to Moscow, bringing her children, Matvei and Anya, with her for a month's visit full of exciting experiences and impressions. It was a joy for us to have them with us, to hear the sound of children's voices in our "duplex" apartment.

Lusia, Ruth, and I lived together for six months after her return; during that time, Ruth became an integral part of our existence. We were hoping that she would remain with us for at least a few more years, but fate decided otherwise.

On December 24, Ruth had supper with us in the kitchen, taking an active part in our conversation about the elections to the Academy. She apparently slept through the night, but in the morning Lusia couldn't waken her. Late on the evening of December 25, Ruth died in her own bed, attended by Lusia and Zora, her niece. Several times on the 25th a faint smile played across her lips, and just before she died, her eyes opened for a moment; and then they closed forever. . . .

Even though she experienced her full share of tragedy, it seems to me that Ruth led a happy life. She preserved her integrity throughout, and

---

*The apartment where the Sakharovs lived had been assigned to Ruth Bonner, Elena Bonner's mother, in 1955. From May 1980, Ruth lived with her grandchildren in Massachusetts.

always found a way to be useful to family, friends, and even strangers. She saw the good in people and the beauty in the world. She was lucky enough to have a daughter like Lusia, and caring family and friends. She had definite opinions, and they were almost always on the mark. Everyone respected her, and many loved her. I felt a special bond with Ruth from the moment I met her in the fall of 1971.*

LUSIA HAS always been close to her children, and separation from them has been a calamity for her and for them. The burden the children carried during the "seven years of Gorky" did not leave them unscathed. I've already written about Alexei. Efrem's professional career was interrupted, and that always creates problems.

The situation with my children from my first marriage† is more difficult and even tragic, especially with my son, Dmitri. He was only fourteen when I remarried. Tanya and Lyuba, my daughters, dissuaded him from living with me, but they too failed to give him the attention he needed. He dropped out during his second year at Moscow University, where he was studying physics, and then, once again, after a single semester of medical school. He hasn't been able to hold a job. How will his life turn out, and that of his son? (Dmitri has already married and divorced.) These are painful questions for me, and, of course, they affect Lusia as well.

What other thoughts did I have a year after my return to Moscow? What hopes for the future?

I dreamed of science. Perhaps I would never accomplish anything of importance. I'd lost too many years, first in work on weapons, then in public activity, and finally in exile in Gorky. Science demands utter concentration, and all these things were distractions. And yet, just being here to see the great advances in high-energy physics and in cosmology is an exhilarating experience that makes life worth living—and of course, there are all sorts of other things in the world that everyone can enjoy.

I expected to maintain at least a nominal interest in some of the undertakings where my name could make a difference: controlled ther-

---

*Sakharov was buried next to Ruth Bonner in Moscow's Vostryakovskoye Cemetery. For more on Ruth, see *Memoirs*, pp. 347–48.
†Sakharov's first wife, Klavdia (Klava) Vikhireva, died in 1969.

monuclear fusion; the underground siting of nuclear reactors; and the use of underground nuclear explosions to control earthquakes.

I realized that Lusia and I would not be able to escape from our civic concerns, even after all the prisoners of conscience were released and large-scale emigration was permitted. We would have to adapt to the challenges that were bound to come while at the same time preserving our integrity.

I HAVE continued to refine my ideas on disarmament and peace. By 1988, I had added a new thesis: since the Soviet army today is much larger than any other army in the world, it would be a significant step forward if we unilaterally cut our term of military service approximately in half, with a simultaneous reduction of all armaments, but without affecting the officer corps in any substantial way. Cutting the term of service is an effective and feasible method of paring down the size of the army, and I am convinced that this would greatly improve the political situation, promote international confidence, create favorable conditions for the complete elimination of nuclear weapons, and generate major social and economic benefits as well.

IN A PREFACE written for *Time*'s publication of my Forum talks, I explained that:

My views were formed during the years I spent on nuclear weapons; in my struggle against testing of these weapons in the atmosphere, underwater, or in space; in my civic activity and writing; in the human rights movement; and in Gorky isolation. My fundamental ideas were expressed in a 1968 essay, *Reflections on Progress, Peaceful Coexistence, and Intellectual Freedom,* but since then life has brought many changes that have forced me to modify my position and respond to altered circumstances. I am referring in particular to recent changes in the domestic life and foreign policy of the USSR.

The main and constant ingredients of my position are the idea that the preservation of peace is indissolubly linked to the openness of society and the observance of human rights, as formulated in the Universal Declaration of Human Rights, and the conviction that only the convergence of the socialist and capitalist systems can assure a fundamental and lasting solution to the problem of peace and the survival of mankind.

3

NEW CIRCUMSTANCES,
NEW PEOPLE,
NEW RESPONSIBILITIES

AFTER A TWO-YEAR INTERVAL, I now [July 1989] have an opportunity to bring my account of events up to date and describe my participation in the most significant event of recent years—the Congress of People's Deputies. During this period, there have been fundamental changes in the thinking of all sections of the population on public issues, and I myself look at many things differently than I did two years ago, or even six months ago.

IN THE SUMMER of 1987 Lusia, Ruth, and I spent a month in Estonia, in a village called Otepya. Galina Yevtushenko,* who owns a house there, found us a very comfortable place—two small rooms with a kitchen. Another family rented the remainder of the house, and someone else lived in the shed. The proprietors owned a second house a few blocks from us as well as a farm outside town, where the landlady's relatives lived. I'm including these details because they give some notion of a way of life that differs greatly from that usually encountered in the Moscow region and in the Russian Republic generally.

This was my first visit to the Baltic Republics, other than brief trips

*Former wife of the poet Yevgeny Yevtushenko, and a long-time friend of Elena Bonner.

to Tallinn for a conference and to Vilnius for Kovalev's trial. Southern Estonia with its numerous lakes and forested hills is lovely. We picked mushrooms and berries, Lusia swam in the lakes and drove Ruth on daily outings. That summer turned out to be Ruth's last, but we have the satisfaction that we spent it the way we did—in the country, free and happy. And, most important, together. A year earlier, that wouldn't have been possible.

We were amazed by Estonia's high standard of living, the organization and tempo of economic activity, the patent contrast to European Russia. We had driven from Moscow in our new car, and after passing through the neighboring Pskov region, where the pothole-ridden roads hadn't been repaired in years, the superior Estonian highways came as a pleasant surprise. We saw neat, well-spaced farmhouses, peasants preparing fodder with *their* mowers for *their* cows (several per farm) and working the fields with *their* tractors. Vats of fresh milk were left under awnings by the side of the road to be picked up by special trucks and taken to the dairy.

We often heard people in Estonia say that they work harder and better, and therefore they live better. That, of course, is only a small part of the truth, the superficial explanation. The deeper reason is that the steamroller of socialism passed over their land later, in a watered-down, rather slipshod fashion: it had less time to do its destructive work. In the "old" Republics that have been part of the USSR from the very beginning, peasants have been debased to a far greater degree—in some instances, they were physically eliminated—and society is more conspicuously divided into separate castes, including a Party bureaucracy, essentially parasitic in nature. It's no accident that leasehold, cooperative, and, especially, private forms of economic activity are developing slowly in those regions, hindered almost openly by local Party and state organs. The Baltic Republics have set an example for our whole country with their popular movements for a genuine, not a fictitious *perestroika* and for a radical resolution of nationality problems through economic autonomy and the adoption of a new compact between the Union and its constituent Republics.

IN THE SUMMER of 1987 the magazine *Teatr* published an interview with me about a new play based on Mikhail Bulgakov's *Heart of a*

Dog. * My first appearance in the Soviet press since the 1960s—despite the somewhat adventitious topic—attracted a lot of attention.

In November, *Moscow News* published a second interview with me ["It's an Absolute Necessity to Speak the Truth: Impressions of the Film *Risk,*" no. 45, November 1987], in which I managed to insert some significant comments. Then came another interview for *Moscow News* ["The Breakthrough Must Be Continued and Widened," no. 49, December 1987], this time on social and political matters: it was the first appearance in print of my recommendation to cut the length of military service in half. (The idea was supported by numerous letters to the editors.) In December 1987, however, an interview I gave to the weekly *Argumenty i fakty,* in which I spoke in some detail about reductions in nuclear weapons, was not printed.†

In October 1987 Lusia and I traveled to Vilnius, where a small group of American and Soviet scientists were meeting to discuss disarmament. The conference had been organized by the Space Research Institute, then headed by Roald Sagdeyev. The chairman of the U.S. delegation, Wolfgang Panofsky, suggested that all work on advanced technologies that could be used to create new weapons (for instance, the development of sophisticated lasers) should be open. He stressed the need for scientific analysis to determine which technologies should come under this provision.

TOWARD THE END of 1987, I agreed to serve as chairman of the Academy's Commission on Cosmomicrophysics and as a director of the International Foundation for the Survival and Development of Humanity. These commitments contradicted my custom of acting as an individual and refusing to accept administrative responsibilities. I have since come to regret them both.

The real organizers of the Commission on Cosmomicrophysics, Mikhail Khlopov and Andrei Linde, assured me that my duties as chairman would be purely honorary and would require no effort on my part. Of

---

*Bulgakov wrote this satire on the Russian Revolution in 1925; it has been translated by Michael Glenny (Harcourt, Brace & World, 1968).

†It was, however, published shortly after Sakharov's death in *Argumenty i fakty,* no. 51, 1989.

course, this was not the case at all, but the work may lead to interesting projects, such as the organization of an international space observatory and the creation of a radiointerferometer with a space base. This might bring me back to something approaching scientific activity (which has long been an impossible dream for me). My work on the baryon asymmetry of the universe played a role in the birth of this new discipline of cosmomicrophysics, which couples the cosmology of the early universe with the physics of elementary particles.

THE BUSINESS with the International Foundation for the Survival and Development of Humanity was a sadder affair. The Foundation was the brainchild of Evgeny Velikhov. (Some credit for the idea should probably also go to his colleague Rustem Khairov.) During the February 1987 Moscow Forum, Velikhov enlisted the help of Jerome Wiesner [president emeritus of MIT] and several other foreigners in planning this venture, and a number of organizational meetings were held in the United States and in Moscow. I learned of the project from Wiesner, who came to our apartment in order to persuade me to join the Foundation; then Khairov reiterated his invitation. I assumed that joining the Board of Directors would be a logical continuation of my previous activity and that I'd be able to support and promote ideas I had been developing over many years. I didn't realize that the Foundation would spend most of its time on administrative and financial functions (as is the case, in fact, for most foundations). This serious misunderstanding was due in part to the utopian picture Wiesner and particularly Khairov drew of the Foundation's prospects and of the opportunities that my participation would generate.

On January 13 and 14, 1988, the Board of Directors rushed through the first organizational meetings in order to keep an appointment with Gorbachev scheduled for the 15th. I learned that Wiesner and Velikhov had recruited a board of thirty members from countries around the world, many more than originally planned, and an extremely unwieldy group in practice (four or five would have sufficed). Still worse, the Foundation's program essentially duplicated activity already underway on disarmament, ecology, and other global issues, and eighteen months later it still had not developed an approach that would justify its grandiloquent name, its initial publicity, or its complex and expensive structure. The vaunted international character of the Foundation—with offices in the USSR, the U.S., and Sweden, employing extravagantly large staffs and requiring excessive travel expenses—did not increase its efficiency, but rather hampered its operation. The Foundation *has* initiated a few useful, small-scale ventures; overall, however, it resembles a typical bureaucratic organization working to feed itself and its people.

I wasn't happy with the Foundation's bylaws and drafted an alternative version. Some of my suggestions were probably not realistic: the directors looked at me as if I were crazy when I suggested that they foot the bill individually for 50 percent of their foreign travel expenses (all the directors enjoy substantial incomes). I have always paid my own way when traveling on business inside the USSR.

On the eve of the first meeting I submitted six proposals to Rolf Björnerstedt, the Foundation's executive director, for possible research grants: (1) the feasibility and consequences of shortening service in the Soviet army; (2) underground siting of nuclear power plants; (3) a draft agreement to ensure that all scientific research that might contribute to the development of particularly dangerous weapons systems would be conducted openly (per Panofsky's suggestion); (4) legal safeguards for freedom of expression; (5) legal safeguards to secure for all persons the free choice of country of residence; (6) humanization of the penitentiary system.

After some delay, the last three topics were approved in principle by the Board of Directors, but the mode of implementation was left vague. In January 1988, I had hopes that the Foundation could influence the drafting of new laws on freedom of expression, freedom of movement, and the penitentiary system by fostering collaboration between those commissioned to carry out the proposed studies and the Institute of State and Law and other bodies charged with preparing the draft laws. These hopes turned out to be unwarranted, since the Institute of State and Law has in fact no direct role in framing the final version of legislation, and it was not realistic to think we could influence things on a higher level. But the wheel of "human rights," so popular in the West, began to spin, pulling in new people. In order to live up to the Foundation's "international character," all three topics were restructured and turned into comparative studies of laws and juridical practice instead of focusing on pending legislation in the Soviet Union. I was made chairman of the Foundation's Human Rights Committee, and a Human Rights Project Group (including Soviet, American, and Swedish members) was organized. On the Soviet side, several dissidents, including Sergei Kovalev and Boris Chernobylsky, joined the Group.

The Foundation's support for these activities was due to Velikhov's and Wiesner's desire to exploit the West's great interest in human rights and my personal popularity for the benefit of the Foundation and its fund-raising activities. All this put me in a false position, especially at a time when "classical" human rights issues are no longer as pivotal as they were a few years ago and when new opportunities for change have opened up in the Soviet Union. The majority of prisoners of conscience have been freed. Emigration has become easier, and progress continues to be made. Other issues, about which we never even dared to think, have come to the fore: the constitutional restructuring of the country and the whole complex of difficulties associated with relations among the nationalities; radical economic reform; a multiparty system; ecological problems; and social questions, including poverty, health, and education.

As a board member, I haven't been expected to monitor the Foundation's activities in detail, but as Chairman of the Human Rights Committee—I'm not quite sure how I acquired that title—I have certain specific responsibilities, which I've fulfilled superficially. This may be unfair to those whom I've involved in this work, but what can I do? I've had neither the strength nor the desire to do more.

For the January 15 meeting with Gorbachev, the Foundation was represented by selected directors and staff, and by several guests invited by Velikhov, Wiesner, and Björnerstedt. We were asked to wait in a room adjacent to the conference room. Gorbachev arrived with his entourage five minutes ahead of schedule, shook hands with everyone, and exchanged a few words with some. I said that I was grateful for his intervention in the fate of my wife and myself. "I received freedom, but simultaneously I feel a heightened responsibility. Freedom and responsibility are indivisible."

"I'm very happy to hear you connect those two words," Gorbachev replied.

After Gorbachev's welcome, we went into the conference room, where Velikhov, Wiesner, some of the rank-and-file directors (including

Dmitri Likhachev and myself), and some of the guests gave brief speeches. I said that the Foundation's significance was linked to its independence from the state apparatus of any country and from organizations pursuing their own specific aims. I recited the research topics I had proposed (except for the underground siting of nuclear reactors, which I mentioned to Gorbachev only later on). I emphasized the advantages of reducing the term of military service. I submitted a list (compiled at my request in December and January but not, unfortunately, as complete or accurate as it might have been) of prisoners of conscience still in labor camps, exile, or psychiatric hospitals. During my talk, I referred to the list and sent it around the table to Gorbachev (we were seated at an oval-shaped marble table, with a marvelous floral centerpiece). One man sitting near me intercepted the paper before it reached its destination, and Gorbachev, noting my surprised look, explained that this was his adviser Ivan Frolov. The list was passed on to the Procuracy of the USSR, and Deputy Procurator General Alexei Vasiliev called me several times concerning it. It may have expedited the release of several prisoners of conscience in 1988.

Gorbachev spoke toward the end of the meeting. Briefly touching on the significance of the Foundation as an international organization created in the spirit of the new political thinking, he devoted most of his presentation to a covert and occasionally overt debate with me and other proponents of more radical changes. Gorbachev stressed the danger of rushing things, of skipping necessary intermediate stages. With respect to a possible reduction in military service, he noted the risk and futility of unilateral acts of disarmament by the USSR, referring to experience with the 1985 moratorium on nuclear tests. (I didn't think the example was very convincing: such a major and unprecedented step as cutting the length of military service in half and moving toward a professional army defies analogy.)

This was my first face-to-face encounter with Gorbachev; he appeared intelligent, self-possessed, and quick-witted in discussion, and the policies he was pursuing at the time impressed me as consistently liberal, fostering a gradual growth of democracy by means of fundamental reforms.

Of course, I wasn't satisfied with the half-measures of the government, several seemingly retrograde actions, and the defects of certain legislation (for instance, the decrees penalizing "unearned" income*), but I attributed these failings mainly to the constraints that inhibit every leader, especially a reformer, and to the rules of the game prevailing in the milieu in which Gorbachev had made his career and in which he was still operating. On the whole, I saw him as the initiator and pace-setter of *perestroika,* and his attitude toward me seemed respectful, even sympathetic.

IN FEBRUARY 1988, Nagorno-Karabakh exploded. Events there exposed the falsehoods of official propaganda extolling the "indestructible friendship of the peoples of our country," and revealed the gravity of interethnic conflicts, which earlier had been kept submerged by terror and censorship. These conflicts, as we know now, affect the entire country.

For over sixty years the Armenians of the Nagorno-Karabakh Autonomous Region [about 70 percent of the region's population] were oppressed by the Azerbaijanian authorities. *Perestroika* encouraged Armenian hopes for a change in this intolerable situation. On February 20, 1988, the regional Soviet of People's Deputies appealed to the Supreme Soviets of Azerbaijan and of Armenia to transfer jurisdiction over Karabakh from the Azerbaijan SSR to the Armenian SSR. Azerbaijan refused, and a pogrom directed against the Armenian inhabitants of Sumgait [a city in Azerbaijan, not far from Baku] followed. The reaction of the country's central leadership continually lagged behind events and appeared inexcusably vacillating and unprincipled. I will go further: official policy still seems unjust, one-sided, and provocative. The central

---

*On May 28, 1986, *Izvestia* published three decrees "On Measures to Reinforce the Struggle Against Unearned Incomes" that triggered an intensive police campaign against various forms of entrepreneurial activity, including the private production and marketing of fruits, vegetables, and other foods. There is no precise definition of the catch-all term "unearned income" (which is prohibited by Article 13 of the USSR Constitution) and its interpretation is left to the court in each case, but the Criminal Codes provide for punishment of so-called economic crimes—including "private entrepreneurial activity," "speculation," and "activity as a commercial middleman"—by lengthy terms of imprisonment. The Swedish economist Anders Åslund believes that the campaign against unearned incomes, which he attributes to Ligachev's influence, seriously undermined public confidence in economic reforms before it petered out in the fall of 1987.

press and television, with few exceptions, turned out to be equally partisan and tendentious. In this critical situation, *glasnost* fell by the wayside (and this default was to be repeated on many similar occasions).

For the first time, I began to think about the negative aspects of the new policies, and what might be causing them. Around March 20 I wrote an open letter to Gorbachev about the Crimean Tatars and about Karabakh. I took one copy to *Moscow News;* I had developed a good contact there in Gennady Zhavoronkov. He immediately passed it on to the editor-in-chief, Egor Yakovlev, whom I also knew. I submitted another copy to the Central Committee's letter department; this was essentially a formality, since Yakovlev had already passed my letter on. The next morning I had a call from the head of *Novosti,* Valentin Falin, who invited me to come in at noon and talk about my letter. He gave me the license number of the car he was sending for me. Soon after I left the apartment, Alexander Yakovlev's secretary phoned from the Central Committee and asked Lusia if I could see him at five o'clock. Lusia expected me to finish my appointment with Falin in time to attend the weekly seminar at FIAN, so she asked Yakovlev's secretary to send a car for me there.

Falin was waiting in his receptionist's office—a rather tall man with an elongated face, well known to the viewers of "Studio 9." He conducted the conversation in a tone of great good will and even a certain confidentiality. He said that fate had made him the adviser to several General Secretaries, beginning with Khrushchev. Either in the last years of Brezhnev or under Chernenko, he had developed major differences with the "boss" and had been forced to leave. That gave him an opportunity to devote himself to scholarship, which was more to his taste: his other work had been difficult, confining, and occasionally unpleasant.

In April 1985 Gorbachev, just elected to the post of General Secretary, invited Falin to return to his role as adviser. Before accepting, he studied Gorbachev's statements and the other available evidence of his intentions; Falin decided he wouldn't have to make public statements or act contrary to his own convictions. He claimed to have been following my activities since 1968 and to have read everything I'd written. He had great respect for me and had more than once defended me from unfair accusations, including those of Khrushchev and Brezhnev (he cited a few examples).

Probably Falin's most interesting observations (although I can't vouch for their accuracy) concerned Gorbachev's role and the state of affairs in the upper echelons of the Party. He told me that ever since his election as General Secretary in April 1985, Gorbachev himself had initiated every major change, without exception, in both domestic and foreign policy, and that he was the author of all programmatic statements issued during his term of office. Falin added the qualifier "unfortunately" (implying, according to my interpretation, that dependence on a single individual opens the way to instability and error). Today I know that Anatoly Lukyanov,* who is closely tied to Gorbachev, plays a major role, but Falin didn't mention his name. The Party is divided into two factions, with opposing views on fundamental issues of principle, but Gorbachev, according to Falin, doesn't want to admit it. He didn't explain whether this was due to Gorbachev's naïveté and overtrustful nature (which is hard to believe, considering the position he holds) or to the tactical considerations of a secretive and calculating politician.

With respect to my letter, the immediate reason for our meeting, Falin stated that within hours of its receipt it had been delivered to Gorbachev, who had read it. Falin urged me not to publish it, or at least to postpone any publicity until after March 26, since strikes, demonstrations, and rallies were allegedly scheduled to take place in Yerevan on that date, making it dangerous to inflame passions further. With respect to Sumgait, Falin said, "We've decided in principle that it's sometimes permissible to delay or cut potentially dangerous news reports, but never to print false information." (This seemed to be an oblique admission that deliberate fabrications, such as the reports on radiation levels after Chernobyl, had been published earlier.) Falin—like Yakovlev a few hours later—defended the official accounts of Sumgait, although it later became evident that they had not been accurate. (I should caution the reader that this chapter was written without benefit of a diary, so I may have attributed to Falin remarks actually made by Yakovlev, and vice versa.)

I never made it to the seminar. Lusia, dressed only in a robe, drove me at top speed to FIAN, where I switched to the black Volga that had

---

*Lukyanov, who in the early 1950s attended law school at Moscow University with Gorbachev, was appointed a Secretary of the Central Committee in January 1987. He was elected Deputy Chairman of the Supreme Soviet in 1989 and Chairman in March 1990.

been sent to pick me up. We rushed, siren blaring, to the Central Committee building on Old Square.

I opened the conversation with Alexander Yakovlev,* a man of medium height, slightly plump, with a round, animated face, and unexpected, quick gestures, by asking, "Why couldn't you have immediately announced that the regional Soviet's demand for the transfer of Nagorno-Karabakh was reasonable and would be satisfied? That would have clarified the situation, and Sumgait would never have happened. Events like that occur only when they can still influence the outcome. Even now it's not too late to remove Karabakh from Azerbaijanian rule."

Yakovlev replied, "The national structure of the state can't be changed in any respect. Any revision would create a dangerous precedent; there are too many flash points where ethnic passions could explode. And besides, the particular case of Nagorno-Karabakh is incredibly complex. The four hundred thousand Armenians living in Azerbaijan are to all intents and purposes hostages. The Caucasus is flooded with arms; they're being brought across the border in great quantities. One match would be sufficient to ignite a firestorm."

From what I'd been told, I countered, the Armenians in Azerbaijan were prepared to accept the risk so long as the central authorities took a firm and unequivocal stand. The Constitution did not pose an insurmountable problem: the next session of the Supreme Soviet could amend it.

Time has shown that Yakovlev was mistaken on several points. Soon after our meeting, in July 1988, and again in January 1989, the central government had to act, but the moves were made too late and therefore solved nothing. The measures taken [Nagorno-Karabakh was placed under the direct rule of the central government] did not touch off an explosion of violence; instead, a fabricated provocation alleging the desecration of a sacred grove in a part of Karabakh populated by Azerbaijanis led to mass savagery and in Baku to a demonstration of 500,000 people inflamed by nationalist and extremist Islamic slogans; more than 130,000 Armenians were forced to flee Azerbaijan. For more than eight months, the Armenians had restrained themselves, but now more than 20 Azer-

---

*Yakovlev was then a Senior Secretary of the Central Committee, and generally considered the most radical reformer among the Party elite.

baijanis were killed and 160,000 fled Armenia as refugees, according to Abdul-Rakhman Vezirov's report to the Congress of Deputies. The number of Armenian refugees is probably similar. A pretext can always be found if there are forces interested in promoting bloodshed and disorder, and things can quickly get out of hand if the central government fails to take action and local authorities provide indirect encouragement. (This seems to have been the pattern of the pogroms that have occurred in Sumgait, Fergana, and elsewhere, although facts are hard to come by, and other considerations may have been at play.)

My conversation with Yakovlev also touched on the situation of the Crimean Tatars. He said that almost all my demands had been met by the state commission [appointed to deal with the Tatar question]. I said that this simply wasn't so: local authorities in the Crimea were maintaining their discriminatory policies. I had asked for a *free* and *organized* return of the Crimean Tatars to their homeland, that is, government assistance for all Tatars who wished to return to the Crimea, not just those considered "deserving" by the authorities. That was the only way to correct the injustice of their deportation. In my letter I hadn't raised the question of restoring an autonomous Crimean Tatar republic, an omission that angered my Crimean Tatar friends and caused several of them to break off relations with me, but in this respect their demands were impractical, if only for demographic reasons. It might be realistic to create a smaller national enclave in the Crimea with a compact settlement there of Crimean Tatars (on a voluntary basis, of course).

I also raised Raoul Wallenberg's case with Yakovlev. Unfortunately, information I had received from Guy von Dardel, Wallenberg's half-brother, that he was being held in a secret camp near the town of Mirny was inaccurate; because of this, my intervention may have inadvertently set back efforts to clarify Wallenberg's fate.*

As our talk drew to a close, Yakovlev asked me what Lusia had done

---

*Wallenberg, a Swedish diplomat who rescued many thousands of Hungarian Jews from the Nazis during World War II, was arrested by Soviet troops soon after they occupied Budapest in 1945. His fate remains mysterious: in 1990, the Soviet authorities, while still insisting that he had died in Moscow's Lubyanka Prison in 1947, finally agreed to let an international commission investigate the matter. For further information on Sakharov's role in the Wallenberg case, see Andrei Sakharov, "The Fate of Raoul Wallenberg," *Moscow News*, No. 37, 1989.

during the war, and when saying goodbye he sent best wishes to the "senior nurse." That concluded my second private conversation with a Politburo member (the first had been with Suslov thirty years before*). I came away from this and subsequent meetings with Yakovlev with the impression that he was an intelligent man, well versed on both domestic and foreign-policy matters, an undoubted supporter of *perestroika* and slightly to the left of Gorbachev. He has no pretensions to the number-one spot, but he can and should be number two. I sensed that Yakovlev (and probably every other *perestroika* activist) has retained an indelible residue of Leninist dogma—it's hard to describe its specific content, but it's there.

IN MARCH 1988, Progress Publishing House asked me to contribute to *Inogo ne dano* (There Is No Alternative), a collection of articles on *perestroika*. Many famous authors were included in the book, which was edited by Yuri Afanasiev, rector of the Historical Archives Institute. We soon came to know him as a man with firm progressive convictions, a bold and imaginative politician. Lusia read my article ("The Inevitability of *Perestroika*") and predicted that it would never be published: it was too daring. (I had insisted on my usual condition that no cuts or changes could be made without my consent; a promise to abide by this stipulation was given to all the authors.) This time Lusia was mistaken, and the book, my piece included, appeared in June, just before the Party Conference. My article was far from the most interesting or venturesome. A few months later, I would have written a quite different article.

We are receiving an education in politics with incredible speed. The spring of 1988 brought home to us the forward thrust of *perestroika*, and of *glasnost* first and foremost, but also the risky, contradictory character of the process. In March, Nina Andreyeva's Stalinist article appeared in *Sovietskaya Rossiya*.† In April, Afanasiev drafted a collective letter, which I signed—even though I knew its objective was quixotic—arguing that the Nineteenth Party Conference [which met in Moscow from June 28 through July 1, 1988] should be postponed for six months in order

---

*See *Memoirs*, pp. 205–207.

†For an English translation of this reactionary manifesto, see David Lane, ed., *Soviet Society Under Perestroika*, Unwin Hyman, 1990, pp. 108–17.

to permit the organization of more democratic elections, since anti-*perestroika* candidates enjoyed enormous advantages.

IN LATE APRIL, Lusia and I left Moscow to spend three weeks at Pitsunda, a resort in Abkhazia on the Black Sea. (We had bought vacation vouchers from the Academy's services department.) Those were marvelous days, free, productive, and happy. Almost no one disturbed us; we were alone together. Our room was tiny, but from the twelfth floor we had a marvelous view of the sea. I worked at the dinner table, while Lusia would type, with her chair in the room and her table on the terrace. That's how we fit.

Lusia began her second book, the story of her childhood before 1937.* I was preparing a talk on the baryon asymmetry of the universe for the conference celebrating the centennial of Alexander Friedmann's birth.† I had to spend time in Moscow and Pitsunda catching up on the extensive recent literature in the field. This review stimulated my thinking; and my talk, I hope, even contained a few new ideas. But the basic question, the specific process that produced the baryon asymmetry of the universe, still isn't clear.

Meals were served in a dining room about two hundred yards from our building (now and again I would go there by myself and bring back something for Lusia). On one occasion, Lusia noticed that our waitress, an Abkhazian woman, was visibly upset. It turned out that she had met a young man who had served a prison term, they were planning to marry, but the chairman of the district executive committee put off registering the marriage on various pretexts. He had called in the husband-to-be for a talk, and the real reason for the chairman's reluctance emerged. The waitress's fiancé wasn't a permanent resident of Pitsunda; he'd been granted permission only for temporary residence as a member of a geological team. If he married a local woman, he would automatically qualify for permanent residence, but in Pitsunda, as in all resort areas, the population is strictly controlled, and there are probably unpublished

---

*Scheduled for publication by Alfred A. Knopf in 1991.
†Friedmann (1888–1925) was a geophysicist and mathematician who applied Einstein's relativity equations to cosmological models.

regulations that caution against the settlement of ex-convicts. I sent the chairman a polite telegram reminding him that no restrictions may be placed on the right to marry except those prescribed by law. The telegram did its work. Soon after, the happy newlyweds brought flowers to our room and thanked us for our assistance.

From Pitsunda we traveled by train along a scenic route to Tbilisi in order to attend a conference on the physics of elementary particles. On this visit, the city of Tbilisi seemed particularly peaceful, festive, and somehow Western in spirit. We admired the balcony of an old house overlooking the Kura River and wondered who lived there: we naturally had no idea that in less than a year's time we would return to Tbilisi and would stay in that very house.

We spent part of June in Leningrad, living and working in an enormous apartment of the House for Visiting Scholars. There was no common dining room; when we tried to buy takeout food at one of the city's more fashionable restaurants, all Lusia could get was semi-edible kasha of a type that neither of us had seen since the war. Food was in short supply in Leningrad, just as in the rest of the country, and the situation isn't getting better.

The conference coincided with a meeting of the International Foundation, and I had to rush from one part of town to the other. After the conference ended, I took part in a round-table on cosmology, and made my first appearance on Soviet television on "The Fifth Wheel," a popular show seen in Moscow as well as in Leningrad. Unfortunately, all my remarks on Nagorno-Karabakh were cut.

A bit belatedly, in July, just before the long-awaited session of the Presidium of the Supreme Soviet devoted to Karabakh, we initiated a campaign urging termination of that region's subordination to Azerbaijan and proposing introduction of an administration responsible only to Moscow. We called several people in Moscow and Leningrad, asking them to send telegrams and to pass along our request to others who shared our views. Several dozen telegrams were probably generated by this initiative, which was Lusia's idea.

Lusia and I also went to see the poet Rasul Gamzatov, who had just arrived in Moscow for the meeting of the Presidium; we called on him in his luxurious home, furnished in Oriental style, and asked him to support our proposal. The conversation was difficult, Gamzatov was

evasive, and Lusia felt our meeting was a waste of time. During the
Presidium debate, however, Gamzatov made an excellent speech. Inci-
dentally, it seemed to us that the younger generation, Gamzatov's
daughter and son-in-law, exert a useful liberal influence in his household.

Our plan wasn't adopted at the time, but it was the central provision
of the so-called "special form of administration" introduced into Karabakh six months later in January 1989; by that time, however, it was not
sufficient to stem the unrest. The resolution passed in July 1988 was
limited to an expression of support for the economic and cultural development of Karabakh in cooperation with Armenia. This would have
been a significant concession back in February, and might then have
successfully defused the tension; but by July people's attitudes had hard-
ened, and the Presidium's resolution was too little and too late. Still, I
believe our telegrams may have had some effect.

The whole country watched the telecast of the Presidium debate; it
had a horribly depressing effect on us, and I think on many others as well.
Gorbachev's approach was overtly prejudiced: it was clear that his mind
was made up and that he favored Azerbaijan. He chaired the meeting
in dictatorial fashion, displaying contempt for dissenting opinions and
often blatantly discourteous, particularly to the Armenian members. He
kept interrupting speakers, and interjecting comments on their remarks.
He cut short the rector of Yerevan University, Sergei Ambartsumian,
and asked, "Who gave you the right to speak for the people?" Ambartsumian turned pale, but managed a dignified response, "My constitu-
ents," and went on with his speech.

We don't know what lay behind Gorbachev's anti-Armenian and
pro-Azerbaijani position, which persisted even after a devastating earthquake struck Armenia. Gorbachev could have turned the Armenians into
the vanguard of *perestroika*, into loyal and hard-working allies. (The
slogans of the first months of the nationalist movement in Armenia
made this plain.) The Armenians would have quickly made up the
production lost through strikes. But Gorbachev chose a different path.
Why? Some say that this was grand strategy, a reflection of the great role
Islam plays in the world and in our own country. Others, like Yakovlev,
attribute it to the fear of new Sumgaits. And still others warn that you
can't create a precedent of territorial change in a country with so many
"hot spots." All these arguments fail to convince me: fundamental

considerations of justice cannot be ignored. Some people ascribe Gorbachev's attitude to supposed links with the Azerbaijanian mafia* or to family ties. Since biographical information on our leaders is hard to come by—*glasnost* does not apply to the highest circles of our society—such rumors flourish, with or without any basis in fact, and it is impossible to either prove or disprove them.

Both before and after the July 18 meeting, I tried to call Gorbachev to explain the idea of "a special form of administration" (the term used then was "presidential rule"). I didn't get through, but his secretary asked me to stay by the phone so that Gorbachev could return my call. We had planned to go away, but we delayed our departure. It was unbearably hot and humid, and our building was undergoing major repairs, which caused us and the other tenants serious inconvenience.

A WEEK LATER, after I came to the conclusion that Gorbachev knew why I was calling and was simply unwilling to speak with me, we finally escaped for three weeks to Protvino, a town about fifty miles south of Moscow, which is the home of the largest particle accelerator in the USSR. I had a long-standing invitation to visit the research center for high-energy physics, and my hosts organized a tour of the vast complex, including the data-processing department. They described the design and capabilities of the powerful accelerator then under construction and their plans for its use. They hoped that this apparatus would be capable of producing two proton beams with an energy of 3 Tev (trillion electron volts) in two accelerator-storage rings, located in a circular underground tunnel thirteen miles long which was being built by a crew experienced in subway construction; in 1988 more than half the work had been completed.

The two proton beams will move in opposite directions, attracted toward the center of the rings by the field produced by special superconducting magnets. The magnets are cooled by liquid helium (the temperature of liquid hydrogen is not low enough for the superconductors now

*In the Soviet Union, the term "mafia" is widely used for any network of people—sometimes, but not always, ethnically based—engaged in the peddling of political influence and favors, and often in overtly illegal activities.

available). The storage rings have common straight-line sections, where the two beams collide with the combined energy of 6 Tev.

In June 1989 when I visited the European Center for Nuclear Research (CERN), the director, Carlo Rubbia, told me that there is a plan to install in Protvino a CERN-developed source of antiprotons, so that one of the colliding beams will be composed of protons and one of anti-protons. This will eliminate the need for two separate rings, making the whole project less expensive and more important, substantially advancing the project's anticipated completion date.

MOST OF THE TIME we spent in Protvino we were free to do as we wished—Lusia continued working on her book, and I kept busy too. In the evenings, we drove out to the picturesque countryside to gather mushrooms, which Lusia fried up.

Our tranquil existence was not without interruptions. Because of the repairs to our building, we had to go back to stifling Moscow for two days. And we received an unexpected visit in Protvino from Yuri Afanasiev, Leonid Batkin, Len Karpinsky, Yuri Karyakin, and two or three other leading members of the liberal Moscow intelligentsia. They wanted to organize a club to engage in critical inquiry into different aspects of *perestroika*—economic, social, legal, ecological, and international. We came up with a name for this forum: the Moscow Tribune. The main argument for organizing such a club, in effect an embryonic legal opposition, was the threatening political situation. There were dangerous symptoms of a shift to the right. New subscriptions to liberal journals and newspapers had been limited; cooperatives had been curbed, and heavy taxes imposed on them; economic reforms had been brought to a virtual standstill; *glasnost* was circumscribed; the Nineteenth Party Conference had been conducted in an undemocratic manner; and the Karabakh question had not been resolved. Subsequently, in July 1988, the adoption of antidemocratic decrees restricting public demonstrations, and granting new and greater powers to the Ministry of Interior's special forces, caused additional concern. At Protvino, we agreed upon a first version of the Moscow Tribune's manifesto, and a few months later the club was formally initiated. Although I agreed to join the Tribune's organizing committee, Batkin and others have played a much greater role in its work. On the whole, after overcoming some initial difficulties, the Moscow Tribune has been an interesting and important undertaking.

EARLIER IN 1988, I had been involved in the turbulent formation of the Memorial Society, another, much larger organization, with an uncertain but potentially substantial prospect of influencing public opinion. Some months before the Nineteenth Party Conference a group of young activists, including Lev Ponomarev, Yuri Samodurov, Vyacheslav Igrunov, Dmitri Leonov, and Arseny Roginsky, called for the creation of a memorial for the victims of illegal repressions—at first, according to my recollection, they spoke only of a monument, and then of an entire complex to include a museum, an archive, a library, and so on. The idea quickly caught on throughout the Soviet Union, and a mass movement developed in support of the enterprise, which was expanded to encompass projects in regions other than Moscow, including the sites of Stalin's principal forced-labor and extermination camps. In addition to its historical and educational tasks, the Memorial Society added the goal of providing legal and moral assistance to those victims of repression who were still alive.

Yuri Afanasiev presented a petition from Memorial with several thousand signatures to the Nineteenth Party Conference. The Conference authorized the erection of a monument to the victims of repression (a similar resolution had been adopted by the Twenty-second Party Congress in 1961,* but it was never implemented); no mention was made of Memorial's other proposals. The movement began to organize, and a number of cultural unions, including the Cinematographers' Union, the Architects' Union, and the Designers' Union, as well as *Literaturnaya gazeta*, agreed to serve as sponsors. A bank account was opened for

---

*Congresses, held at approximately five-year intervals, are the supreme governing bodies of the Communist Party. Gorbachev decided to convene an all-Union Conference, second in the hierarchy of Party forums, to energize the Party's ranks without waiting for the next Congress. Both the Nineteenth Party Conference, convened in June 1988, and the Twenty-eighth Party Congress, convened in July 1990, were dominated by conservatives who blocked many of Gorbachev's proposals.

donations to the Memorial Society and for the proceeds realized from special concerts, lectures, and films. At this stage, a poll was taken on Moscow's streets: passersby were asked to name those they would like to see on Memorial's Council, and those who received the greatest number of votes were invited to serve on the Society's governing body. I was among them, and I accepted my nomination, as did the majority who received the public's endorsement.

Alexander Solzhenitsyn declined. In December 1988, while in the United States, I called him to extend congratulations on his seventieth birthday. During our conversation, Solzhenitsyn explained his action. He mentioned first of all the decision to exile him from his homeland in retaliation for *The Gulag Archipelago*. This was illogical, since Memorial could hardly be held responsible for the actions of the Soviet authorities. His second argument was his fear that Memorial's ideological line would clash with his own historical concepts. Expanding on this thought, he said that he was absolutely against limiting criticism to Stalinist repressions, or, still worse, focusing on the repression of those who were in fact accessories to the crimes of the regime, crimes which had begun in 1917 and continued to this day. The physical destruction of the people and their best representatives, the corruption of the population, the deceit, cruelty, hypocrisy, and demagoguery engaged in for the sake of power and the false goals of Communism were links in a single chain of events that had been initiated by Lenin. His personal guilt before the people and history was enormous, but discussion of Lenin's crimes was still a taboo subject in the USSR, and so long as that remained true, Solzhenitsyn wanted no part of Memorial.

He ended the conversation by extending his best wishes for my success in the struggle I was waging inside the USSR, taking into account the prevailing circumstances and opportunities. Of course, I am paraphrasing Solzhenitsyn's remarks from memory, augmenting them with fragments from his public statements and interpreting them in the light of my own experience. What can I reply to Solzhenitsyn's criticism? The necessity for expanding Memorial's terms of reference beyond the Stalin period, for more clearly defining Memorial's ideological platform, comes up repeatedly. Nevertheless, it is important to bear in mind that Memorial is a mass organization, formed on the basis of certain specific ideas and aims shared by all its members; on all other issues, mutual tolerance has to be the rule. Furthermore, Memorial has to function in the conditions of Soviet reality, and the official attitude toward it is wary, if not openly hostile. Therefore, I favor the cautious formulation contained in the bylaws that speaks of "the victims of Stalinist repressions and other victims of state terrorism and illegal government acts." The reactions of the Central Committee and other official instances and the difficulties Memorial has encountered in registering as an organization have made it clear enough that the authors of the bylaws and Memorial as a whole have not succumbed to conformity.

THIS SEEMS the appropriate place to complete the story of my December 1988 conversation with Solzhenitsyn. I called from Newton in the morning. His wife, Natalya, answered the phone. We spoke for several minutes before she called Solzhenitsyn, noting that this was an exception, since he almost never comes to the phone himself. After completing the conversation about the Memorial Society and in response to his wishes for success, I said a few words about the importance of his work as a writer, and then added, "Alexander Isayevich, there should be nothing left unsaid between us. In your book *The Oak and the Calf* you hurt me deeply, insulted me. I'm speaking of your pronouncements about my wife, sometimes explicit and sometimes without naming her, but it's perfectly clear whom you mean. My wife is absolutely not the person you depict. She's an infinitely loyal, self-sacrificing, and heroic person, who's never betrayed anyone. She keeps her distance from all salons, dissident or otherwise, and she's never imposed her opinions on me."

Solzhenitsyn was silent for several seconds—he probably wasn't accustomed to direct rebukes. Then he said, "I would like to believe that it is so." By ordinary standards, that wasn't much of an apology, but for Solzhenitsyn it was apparently a major concession.*

IN THE FALL of 1988 I made my first speech at a public meeting. It was convened by Memorial near the Palace of Sports of the Roadbuilding

---

*For the background of this exchange, see *Memoirs*, pp. 399–404, and Solzhenitsyn's *The Oak and the Calf* (Harper & Row, 1980).

Institute. Lusia drove me there but didn't attend, since she had to park too far from the rally to walk there with her bad legs. The crowd—there were several hundred people, perhaps more than a thousand—recognized me, and I said a few words after several others had spoken. Of course, I had nothing prepared, but I think it went well in contrast to my next appearance, at the Memorial conference in October, where I was the first orator and read a prepared text. It was shamefully boring.

This was supposed to be the founding conference, which would adopt the bylaws and announce the creation of the all-Union Memorial Society, but about a week before the meeting was scheduled, the Central Committee began objecting to it on several farfetched pretexts. In particular, Yudin, an official in the Central Committee, assembled the secretaries of our sponsoring unions and frightened them into asking the Executive Committee to postpone the conference. In fact, the Central Committee didn't like the idea of an independent mass public organization, one that would be hard to control and that included many celebrities among its members. The Executive Committee wanted to avoid a rift with our financial sponsors, so with the sanction of Memorial's Council, the character of the impending gathering was altered. It was too late to cancel it altogether since delegates from all over the country were converging on Moscow.

The founding conference was rescheduled for December 17, but it had to be delayed once again; it finally took place toward the end of January. By then, Memorial was under attack on another front—its representatives were denied access to the organization's bank account in mid-December. This was probably also Yudin's doing, but the formal excuse given was that Memorial was not officially registered. In January, a week before the conference was scheduled to open, members of Memorial's Council, including Afanasiev, Baklanov (the editor of the liberal journal *Znamya*), and Yevtushenko, were summoned to the Central Committee. I wasn't invited, but the others announced that they wouldn't go without me, and at the last moment Lev Ponomarev picked me up in his car. On the way to the meeting, he explained the situation with the bank account, and warned me that we would undoubtedly be pressed to postpone the founding conference once again. But we couldn't put it off any longer. The situation was dangerous for members of local Memorial chapters. We should declare that if we were not allowed the use of a meeting hall we would hold the conference in private apartments. I agreed completely with Ponomarev. He left me at the entrance to the Central Committee's building, and I went upstairs.

The meeting was chaired by Alexander Degtyarev, an assistant to Vadim Medvedev, Alexander Yakovlev's successor as the Central Committee secretary in charge of ideology. Medvedev had brought in Degtyarev from Leningrad, where he'd been a supporter of the Russian nationalist association Pamyat, or so I was told. At first, Degtyarev conducted himself very aggressively. He announced that Memorial did not have the right to the money on deposit in the bank, since a decree adopted by the Central Committee and the Council of Ministers soon after the Nineteenth Party Conference assigned the Ministry of Culture the task of creating a monument to the victims of Stalinist repressions, and therefore all funds collected for this purpose belonged to it.

The members of the Council argued the point energetically, saying that the money had been collected specifically for the Memorial Society; all the contributors knew that and notices to that effect had appeared in the press. Handing over the money to the Ministry of Culture would be totally illegal and would provoke a storm of protest.

Degtyarev changed his tone a bit and said that Memorial couldn't have a bank account since it wasn't registered. And then he told us that commissions attached to the district executive committees (in other words, controlled by official bureaucrats) would be created to study Stalinist crimes. Local Memorial groups could join these commissions, and thus there was no need for a Memorial Society or a founding conference. Degtyarev's assistant added that the draft bylaws were juridically unsound and that he, as a Communist, was shocked that they didn't contain the word "socialism."

We replied forcefully, sensing danger. I said that an official commission and a public organization were very different things. The significance of a public organization lies precisely in its independence, and we would never agree to lose that independence. If we were refused recognition and a meeting hall, we would hold the conference in private apartments (I was following Ponomarev's advice). As for the word "socialism," the bylaws are not the Party program and are not the appropriate place for theoretical discussions.

Leaving the meeting, I asked Afanasiev, "Well?" (I meant our prospects in general and the position of the Central Committee in particular, and Afanasiev, of course, understood my question in that way.)

He replied, "Very bad."

Apparently, however, this was just one last psychological attack before the authorities made a decision, and we withstood it. Such rearguard actions are standard practice, and we've encountered them many times.

On the eve of the conference, Vadim Medvedev invited me back to his Central Committee office. We discussed the same topics, but in a much friendlier tone. When I got home, I learned that the Central Committee had stopped the printing of *The Memorial Herald*, a newspaper we were planning to hand out at the conference. The reason was the inclusion of two "seditious" pieces—my election program and a demand that Solzhenitsyn's Soviet citizenship be restored and *The Gulag Archipelago* be published.

I called Degtyarev first and then Medvedev, and I spoke very sharply, for me (Lusia says she had never heard me like that). "Is it a prohibition or a recommendation?" I asked. "If it's a prohibition, then you're assuming a grave responsibility. If it's a recommendation, then we don't have to follow it."

Medvedev replied, "We're not forbidding you to publish whatever you want, that's not our function, but our attitude toward Memorial will depend on your actions."

I said, "We've taken that into account and have decided to publish our journal as planned. Just cancel the ban against printing it!"

Medvedev said, "We didn't issue such a ban."

"You know perfectly well that's not so! Cancel the ban!"

Medvedev didn't reply. But twenty minutes later they started printing again. However, it turned out that Afanasiev had agreed the night before to take out the material on Solzhenitsyn: the space where it was to have appeared was left blank. The founding conference endorsed the decisions of the organizing committee.

I had another telephone conversation with Medvedev in April 1989. Four women in Ivanovo were conducting a hunger strike, demanding the return of a church confiscated in the 1930s and turned into a warehouse. I called Medvedev and asked him to intercede. He replied that he knew nothing about it. However, someone from the Central Committee—I don't know whether it was before or after my intervention—called the Ivanovo Party Committee and ordered them not to give in to the "extremists" (this epithet figured in local press accounts of the incident) under any circumstances. Using chicanery and threats, they forced the women to abandon their strike. The chairman of the Committee on Church Affairs, who tended to be responsive to religious believers, was soon forced to retire (but other factors may have been involved).

Memorial's status has remained shaky. The all-Union Memorial Society has been refused registration on the grounds that the only legislation regulating the registration of public organizations, passed in 1932, applies only to local organizations, not to national ones. All existing national organizations have been created by specific decrees of the government and purportedly do not need to be registered. Thus the Memorial Society still is denied access to its principal bank account. Some local chapters and their members have been harassed. A few Memorial members wanted to picket the Presidium of the Supreme Soviet, and we barely managed to talk them out of it. I spoke about Memorial with Medvedev and Lukyanov during the June 1989 session of the Congress of Deputies, and they said that the new Supreme Soviet will pass a law on registration sometime soon. But who knows when that will be? And they could deliberately make the new law incompatible with Memorial's bylaws.*

IN OCTOBER 1988, I took part for the first time in a Pugwash Conference† at the invitation of Vitaly Goldansky, director of the Semyonov Institute of Chemical Physics and chairman of the Soviet Pugwash committee. Lusia was also invited. The conference took place in Dagomys, not far from Sochi. The participants and guests were housed in a fashionable Intourist hotel. The meetings took place there, too. The Conference organizers paid all expenses, including travel and room and board for the participants, but Lusia bought her own ticket. The beach and pool were at our disposal, and in the evenings there were cocktail parties with an abundance of free whiskey and vodka; some of the guests went a bit overboard.

Lusia and I attended the plenary sessions and workshops on ecology,

---

*As of August 1990, a draft law on nongovernmental associations has been published, but has not yet been adopted. The all-Union Memorial Society has still not been registered, although many local chapters *have* received such official recognition.

†Pugwash is one of the oldest and most influential international conference series devoted to issues of peace and disarmament.

strategic arms reduction, the balance of conventional arms in Europe, prohibition of chemical weapons, verification of disarmament agreements, controls on nuclear testing, and development in the Third World. My attitude is that, given the critical nature of global problems, Pugwash is worthwhile so long as its efficiency is greater than zero—even if not all that much greater. The mediocre quality of the proceedings—especially the discussions on ecology—may well stem from the fact that many participants were "professionals" in the fight for peace, for the environment, for disarmament, for you-name-it, which does not foster an objective, scholarly approach. What disappointed me even more was that Pugwash seemed so self-absorbed, without a direct link to government or to the media. No doubt some indirect benefits are achieved through the participants' personal contacts in scientific and political circles, so let Pugwash do its work. But without me!

At the Dagomys conference, responding to the speech of the movement's secretary, I emphasized ecological problems, and in particular the danger to the genetic pool caused by the chemicalization of life on earth.

Lusia proposed an interesting approach for saving the rain forests: she suggested that all states earmark a small percentage of their gross national product for countries that would agree to stop destroying their forests and start restoring them. This would constitute an equitable payment for oxygen, for life itself. The amounts should be sufficient to induce both governments and private citizens to preserve the rain forests. Lusia's idea has not received the support it deserves.

BACK IN JUNE I had been invited to take part in a round table at the journal *XX Century and Peace* on the rapprochement of the capitalist and socialist systems. I prepared my remarks in advance, and I think it went well. I spoke of the interconnectedness of global problems and argued that only convergence on the basis of pluralism can guarantee man's survival. It's foolish now to argue whether convergence is possible or not—it's happening already, and in the socialist world it's taking the form of *perestroika*. "Pluralism Is Convergence," the article I wrote for the round table, was published in the January 1989 number of *XX Century and Peace.*

I took part in another round table in November 1988, organized by the magazine *Ogonyok*, on political, cultural, and economic aspects of *perestroika.* There were both American and Soviet participants, but the latter were more knowledgeable.

Twice during the fall of 1988, the editors of *Novy mir* asked for my assistance. The first occasion concerned the publication of Grigory Medvedev's "Chernobyl Notebook," a documentary account written by an atomic-power specialist who had worked at the Chernobyl plant and who revisited it shortly after the accident. I wrote a preface for Medvedev's piece [*Novy mir,* no. 6, June 1989]. Publication of the article was vigorously opposed by bureaucrats who had some responsibility for Chernobyl. I signed a letter to Gorbachev that had been drafted by Sergei Zalygin, the editor-in-chief of *Novy mir,* urging publication of the "Chernobyl Notebook." (I rarely sign documents I haven't drafted myself, but I made an exception in this case, even though I found the letter's style somewhat alien.)

The second occasion involved Solzhenitsyn's *The Gulag Archipelago.* Zalygin wanted to serialize Solzhenitsyn's masterpiece in *Novy mir,* beginning with the January 1989 number, and an announcement to that effect was printed on one of the magazine's covers. But the political situation at the top had changed, and the Central Committee ordered Zalygin to cancel publication. He refused, but instructions were sent directly to the printer, and most of the covers with the offending advertisement were destroyed. That's the way "telephone government" works. This time, Zalygin and I sent a joint letter, again addressed to Gorbachev.

In both cases, the negative decisions were reversed, but we will probably never learn whether this was due to another shift of political direction or to our letters.

In October 1988 Evgeny Feinberg came to sound me out about my availability for nomination to the Presidium of the Academy of Sciences. This was actually Sagdeyev's initiative; for some reason he was unwilling to approach me about it himself. Feinberg said it was very important to have someone in the Presidium who could restrain the current members from committing all sorts of outrages. I said I'd think it over, but I was inclined to accept, since it was more significant than my role in the International Foundation and less of a burden. Naturally, I discussed it with Lusia, who was rather negative toward the idea.

The next day I told Feinberg that I was available. Soon afterward Sagdeyev himself called, and I gave him the go-ahead. He thanked me for my decision, adding that he had been nominated to the Presidium but for a variety of reasons couldn't serve and wished to propose my candidacy instead. Sagdeyev didn't mention Feinberg at all.

A few days later, on October 20, by-elections were held to replace members of the Presidium who had reached the newly imposed mandatory retirement age of seventy. Sagdeyev declined to run, and was greeted with applause from the hall when he placed my name in nomination. In doing so, however, he embarrassed Academician Andrei Gaponov-Grekov, another candidate for the Presidium, who a few days earlier had ceded his place to Sagdeyev but was not prepared to withdraw in my favor. Gaponov-Grekov's name remained on the ballot, but in the end he called on everyone to cross out his name and vote for me instead. Although more than eighty people voted against me, I got a majority. Academician Nikolai Vorontsov [now chairman of the State Committee for the Protection of the Environment, created in January 1988] was also elected to the Presidium, a hopeful sign.

At my first meeting as a member of the Presidium, I zeroed in on the selection of a new director for the Institute of Water Management. This Institute and its former director were responsible for many ecological crimes, and it wasn't clear just where the new director stood. At my suggestion, seconded by Vorontsov, the Presidium discussed this question at another meeting (unfortunately, in my absence). Later on, I tried to change the Presidium's positions on several key issues, organizational and substantive. I recall, in particular, discussions on the wisdom of constructing the Volga-Chograi Canal and the Crimean Atomic Energy Plant, debate on the appointments of directors for certain of the Academy's institutes, and the fierce struggle over the election of People's Deputies from the Academy. Unfortunately, I'm not very good at organizing support and publicity, but I keep hoping that I'll succeed in doing something useful.

4

TRAVEL ABROAD

ON OCTOBER 20, the same day I was elected to the Academy's Presidium, the Politburo lifted the ban on my travel abroad. The International Foundation's officers were extremely interested in getting permission for me to travel. Velikhov had twice appealed to Gorbachev by letter and finally mentioned the matter to him personally during a reception for the President of Brazil, and Gorbachev promised to put the question to the Politburo. But probably the decisive stroke was when Yuli Khariton,* at Velikhov's request, vouched for me in writing (I believe he repeated his endorsement orally at the Politburo meeting of October 20). Khariton may have said that I couldn't possibly know anything of interest after twenty years of exclusion from top-secret work or that I was a person who could be trusted never under any circumstances to reveal state secrets, but, whatever it was, it did the trick. This was definitely an uncommon act of civic courage on Khariton's part, which demonstrated personal trust in me.

On November 6, I traveled abroad for the very first time in my life, in order to attend a board meeting of the International Foundation in Washington, D.C. I also made numerous personal appearances at fundraising meetings; Jerome Wiesner set great store by such activity, and the Foundation was energetically seeking contributors, since its travel

---

*The research director of the "Installation," where Sakharov worked on thermonuclear weapons from 1948 to 1968.

expenses kept it perpetually on the verge of bankruptcy. It needed moral support as well, and many people told me that the Foundation's authority depended on my participation.

I made this first trip without Lusia. We had said many times that we were not requesting permission to travel abroad together, so as not to complicate the authorities' decision. Now we couldn't renege on our words. Besides, Lusia needed to work on her book of childhood memoirs. After my departure, she had to spend several days battling for permission for Kovalev, Chernobylsky, and other members of the human rights group to attend the Washington meeting. The Foundation's Moscow staff turned out to be helpless when it came to this sort of administrative work.

As soon as I landed in New York, and later that evening at the Boston airport, I was met by hordes of reporters with flashbulbs and microphones. At a press conference in Boston, I spoke about the contradictory character of the processes taking place in our country, about the changes in the constitution and the electoral process, about the Crimean Tatars and Nagorno-Karabakh, and about some of the remaining prisoners of conscience. These became recurrent themes in public appearances on my trips abroad. At fund-raising events, I spoke of my doubts regarding the International Foundation: at a reception at the Metropolitan Museum of Art, I compared the Foundation to the centipede that had so many legs—I was thinking of the directors and staff—that it didn't know which foot to start off with and consequently didn't move at all. (At least this occasion allowed my stepdaughter Tanya and me to see the marvelous Degas exhibition then at the Metropolitan.) Velikhov and Wiesner had hoped to raise $10 million for the Foundation, but they got very little—less than a million—from our tour. Wiesner was disappointed by my approach to fundraising, but I had to say what I thought.

I, in my turn, was disappointed by the board meeting. There were no interesting discussions. The only new topic introduced was the development of a mechanism to destroy nuclear-armed missiles in case of an accidental launch. This matter, however, can be dealt with effectively only by diplomats and the engineers who actually work on missiles and on command, control, and communications systems. The Foundation did decide to create and support a Human Rights Project Group, but

I am discouraged by the academic character of its program and distressed by the exaggeration of its significance. Perhaps I am missing something?

IN MY MEETINGS with President Reagan, President-elect Bush, Secretary of State Shultz, and Prime Minister Thatcher, there were many questions on human rights. I seem to be reaping the fruits of my activity in the 1970s and 1980s. My conversations with Shultz and Thatcher focused on the conditions that the West should set for holding an international conference on human rights in Moscow.

Reagan was a charming host. I tried to talk to him about SDI in the broad framework of international strategic stability and disarmament, but he somehow managed to ignore my arguments and repeated his usual claim—that SDI will make the world a safer place.

Unfortunately, I heard the same thing from Edward Teller [the physicist who directed the U.S. H-bomb program]. I met him on his birthday, and we spoke for thirty minutes in relative privacy just before a formal banquet was held in his honor in the ballroom of a Washington hotel. I said a few words about the parallels in our lives, about the respect I had for the principled and determined manner in which he defended his views, regardless of whether I agreed with them or not. (I repeated these thoughts publicly in my speech at the banquet.) Teller spoke about nuclear energy; we had no disagreements on that subject, and we quickly found a common tongue.

I turned the conversation to SDI, since my main reason for coming to see him was to discover the basis of his support for this concept. As I understood it, the moving force behind his promotion of SDI is a profound and uncompromising distrust of the Soviet Union. Technical difficulties can always be overcome if need be—they can and will be solved now that a system of defense from Soviet missiles has been put on the agenda. A shield is better than a sword. Behind all this there was the unspoken thought: We have to develop this defense first. You're trying to scare us off, to sidetrack us, while you've been working in secret on the same idea for years. We were summoned to the banquet before I had a chance to reply.

Tanya was waiting and warned me, "You have exactly fifteen minutes for your speech, otherwise we'll miss the last shuttle." I managed to say everything I wanted to: I spoke for five minutes on fate and sticking to principle; five minutes on the role of MAD (Mutual Assured Destruction); and five minutes on the military, economic, and technological futility of SDI—it would merely raise the threshold of strategic stability.

I also said that SDI fosters escalation from conventional to nuclear warfare, adds to the uncertainty of the strategic and scientific situation, thereby encouraging dangerous and desperate adventures, and complicates disarmament negotiations. At the end of my talk, Tanya and her husband, Efrem, grabbed me and whisked me out of the room. I barely had time to say goodbye to Teller and wave to the audience. Later, one newspaper published an article saying that Sakharov had been hustled away by KGB agents assigned to him. As we were leaving, an officer in full-dress uniform decorated with medals and ornamental cords greeted me and wished me luck: it was Lieutenant General James Abrahamson, director of the SDI program.

WHEN I MET with Bush, I discussed the importance of an American undertaking not to initiate nuclear warfare. At the same time, the USSR should confirm its existing pledge of no first use in a constitutionally binding form. This would create an atmosphere of trust and facilitate arriving at strategic equilibrium in conventional weapons. The idea that nuclear weapons could be employed to halt a conventional-arms offensive creates an illusory sense of security. Nuclear warfare would be equivalent to the suicide of the human race: no one would take the risk of beginning it, since escalation would be inevitable, and there would be no way to stop it. Threats involving a weapon that will never be used are simply not credible. And the false efficacy attributed to Mutual Assured Destruction has encouraged Western neglect of conventional weapons.

Bush took a photograph out of his pocket—several generations of his family posed on some cliffs by the sea—and said, "Here's the guarantee that we'll never use nuclear weapons first. This is my family, my wife, children, and grandchildren. I don't want them to die. No one on earth wants that."

I replied, "If you'll never make first use of nuclear weapons, you should announce that publicly, write it into law." Bush was silent.

I had too many other meetings and conversations in Washington and New York to list them all, but my talk at the Kennan Institute, chaired by Peter Reddaway, was particularly interesting for me.*

After my visit to Washington, I tried to avoid official meetings and alternated between Tanya and Efrem's home in Newton and Liza and Alexei's home in Westwood, spending my time with the children and grandchildren. This was the first time I had seen Sasha, the daughter of Liza and Alexei. I liked her very much—she was lively, smart, bold, and at the same time gentle and cuddly. Sasha's appearance in the world, may I remind the reader, had been made possible by our struggle for Alexei's reunion with Sasha's future mother.† (Can you say that? It was Sasha who was future, after all.)

During that second, quiet part of my stay, I worked hard on my *Memoirs*. I took time out to meet with members of Amnesty International and I filmed a television interview for their campaign against the death penalty.

At this time the Azerbaijani-Armenian conflict flared up again. The situation in Kirovabad was particularly serious, with hundreds of women and children seeking refuge from pogroms and violence in a church that was defended by soldiers reportedly armed only with entrenchment tools. The soldiers behaved courageously, and several were killed.

In Moscow, Lusia received reports through different, seemingly independent channels that a large number of Armenians had been murdered. (Later we learned that these reports were all coming from a single source who was, to put it charitably, not entirely trustworthy.) She passed this information on to me by phone, and I in turn relayed it to President Mitterrand, who was visiting Moscow. I also cited the exaggerated death toll in a public statement. I've made several regrettable mistakes of this sort in recent years—at the least, I should have avoided the use of specific numbers.

---

*A partial transcript of Sakharov's remarks was published in *The New York Review of Books*, December 22, 1988. Peter Reddaway was then director of the Kennan Institute for Advanced Russian Studies.

†In 1981, by conducting a seventeen-day hunger strike, Sakharov and Bonner won permission for Liza Alexeyeva to join Bonner's son, Alexei Semyonov, in the United States. Semyonov had emigrated in 1978 and had married Liza in a proxy wedding ceremony in Montana. (See *Memoirs*, pp. 552–75.)

In early December, Mikhail Gorbachev visited the United States. He delivered a major speech at the UN General Assembly announcing the decision of the Soviet government to reduce its armed forces by 10 percent, and to pull back troops from Eastern Europe. This, of course, was an exceptionally important announcement, an act of statesmanlike courage, but I believe a much deeper cut in our armed forces is possible, with incomparably greater benefits for both domestic and foreign policy. I am continuing my campaign for a 50 percent cut, which can best be accomplished by reducing the term of military service. Just today [summer 1989], as I'm writing these lines, I've heard that the Supreme Soviet has voted to demobilize students inducted in 1988 (young men in this category weren't drafted in 1989). This is wonderful news. Ivan Rekubratsky, my cousin Masha's son, should be among those released.

On December 7, 1988, a severe earthquake in Armenia killed thousands of persons and caused enormous destruction. Gorbachev cut short his trip, flying from New York to Moscow, and then on to Armenia.

President Mitterrand had invited me to a formal celebration of the fortieth anniversary of the Universal Declaration of Human Rights, and I flew into Paris on the morning of December 9, accompanied by Ed Kline and his wife, Jill. (As soon as I'd learned of the earthquake in Armenia, I'd written an appeal for international assistance, which I handed out to reporters on my arrival.) Irina Alberti, the editor-in-chief of the Russian-language newspaper *Russkaya mysl*, was at the airport. Lusia had known her since 1975 and was on good terms with her. There was to be a press conference at the Soviet Embassy on the morning of December 9, and I invited Irina to attend; she agreed, noting that this would be her first visit to the Soviet Embassy.

I was the center of attention at the press conference, although there were other Soviet participants—Fyodor Burlatsky* and several members of his Commission for International Cooperation on Humanitarian Problems and Human Rights who were also in Paris for the anniversary celebration. I said the same things I always say, perhaps a bit more bluntly than usual. I cautioned that in dealing with the USSR, Westerners would have to keep their eyes open in order to make sure that their

---

*Then the chief political analyst for, and currently editor-in-chief of, *Literaturnaya gazeta*.

cooperation promoted *perestroika* and supported the new forces in the USSR. Subsequently, Burlatsky pretended to summarize my remarks, but twisted them into an assertion that the West should assist *perestroika* in every way possible and unconditionally. I had to interrupt and say that the policy I advocated was just the opposite—not unconditional long-term support, but rather an unequivocal stand that any retreat from *perestroika* would mean the end of cooperation between the West and our country.

A doctor from the Burlatsky Commission described the abysmal state of pediatrics in the USSR—the high rate of infant mortality, the lack of drugs, of good hospitals, of disposable syringes, and so on. I was asked at the press conference about psychiatry in the USSR, and in responding to the question, I had an opportunity to correct the error I had made in "The Inevitability of *Perestroika*" when I wrote that "The use of psychiatry for political purposes is a particularly cruel and dangerous practice, notwithstanding the fact that the majority of victims of psychiatric repression are individuals who need psychiatric care." (Alexander Podrabinek* had sent two letters to *Russkaya mysl* criticizing my statement.) Without having exact and representative statistics, I should never have made such a sweeping assertion, based only on my personal impressions, about the mental health of a whole category of people.

ON MY FIRST afternoon in Paris, I made a small tour of the city, accompanied by Ed, Jill, and my French security men. We visited the Cathedral of Notre Dame, an astonishing creation of the human hand and spirit. I can imagine what people in the twelfth or thirteenth century felt when they saw the great vaulted ceilings rising upward, so different from their everyday surroundings. Of course, I had read Victor Hugo as a child, and scenes from his book were still vivid in my mind.

That evening, I was interviewed on the popular French channel Antenne-2, and then went to meet Lusia, who was flying in from Moscow at the invitation of Danielle Mitterrand, the President's wife.

The next morning, I had a private meeting with Lech Walesa; he too

---

*Podrabinek, a paramedic, served more than five years in labor camp and internal exile for writing *Punitive Medicine* (Karoma Publishers, 1980), an exposé of Soviet psychiatric abuses. He now edits *Express-Chronicle*, a weekly Moscow news bulletin.

had come to Paris for the celebrations. Then Lusia and I had substantive, informal discussions with France's Premier Michel Rocard and President François Mitterrand. We were received as guests of the Republic, with a rendition of the "Marseillaise" and impressive ceremony. It was hard to maintain a straight face as we walked between two ranks of guardsmen in dress uniform, with swords unsheathed.

We discussed the need for international assistance after the earthquake in Armenia, Nagorno-Karabakh, and the fate of the Kurds in Iraq. The last topic was one we felt we had to bring up, since we knew that Iraq was deploying against the Kurds soldiers freed by the ceasefire with Iran, and we were especially disturbed by the announcement that poison gases had been used against Kurdish villages. Premier Rocard and President Mitterrand both acknowledged that France—which has close ties with Iraq—was concerned by the events in Iraqi Kurdistan. Rocard expressed doubts about the reported use of poison gas (Mitterrand did not), and said that the problem was a delicate one, involving complex international interests. The leader of the Iraqi Kurds had allegedly collaborated with Iran during the war. Rocard and Mitterrand assured us that a decision had been made, or was about to be made, to cut off military assistance to Iraq, but the imposition of additional sanctions would be difficult.

That afternoon there was a solemn ceremony at the palace of Chaillot, followed by a state dinner. I sat next to Madame Mitterrand, who discussed her plans to aid the Armenian earthquake victims. Lusia, who was placed between Mitterrand and Pérez de Cuéllar, explained the Armenian-Azerbaijanian conflict to the UN Secretary General. The interpreter was busy helping me, and Lusia was exhausted after speaking English for an hour and a half. At the end of the dinner, Pérez de Cuéllar came over to our table and said that if Lusia had briefed him about Armenia before his meeting with Gorbachev in New York he could have questioned him in detail on the subject, but he'd known nothing at the time. Later Alexei [Semyonov] expressed doubts about his professed lack of knowledge, since the Secretary General had been sent abundant material on Karabakh by Armenian organizations.

On December 11, we went sightseeing in Paris. Lusia had spent a month there in 1968, and she'd been free to go wherever she wished. This time we were hemmed in by security, but we managed to visit Montmartre and the Basilica of Sacré-Coeur and to observe the famous street artists. We wanted to go to Place Pigalle and buy Lurex stockings for our fashion plates back in Moscow, but our escorts wouldn't allow it, afraid of crowds and criminals. And in fact, when walking down a neighboring street, we saw a group of young men loitering in an entry-way, hands in their pockets, where I could well imagine them grasping their brass knuckles, switchblades, and other lethal weapons. We bought the stockings in a wildly expensive store, but they weren't quite what we wanted. As we drove through a district filled with sex shops and porno movies, we caught sight of a familiar couple strolling peacefully down the street. It was the gifted balladeer Bulat Okudzhava, Lusia's long-time friend, and his wife. We had to go all the way to Paris to see them. . . .

We had lunch in an Italian restaurant with Irina Alberti and Cornelia Gerstenmaier, editor of the German edition of *Kontinent,* who had come from Bonn to see us. That evening we met with French mathematicians and physicists: the French had helped us more than most in our difficult years, and I am profoundly grateful to them. It was nice to be among friends. Yuri Orlov* came, too. We had an interesting talk about the situation in the Soviet Union and where it was headed. We also had a reunion with our friend Vladimir Maximov, editor of the émigré journal *Kontinent.* He was, as usual, battling "rhinoceroses" and their accomplices and the accomplices of their accomplices. We started talking about Gorbachev. Maximov said, "The KGB studied their man, calculating his assets and liabilities from their perspective. Now there's no alternative to Gorbachev."

---

*A physicist and human-rights activist who founded the Moscow Helsinki Group, and was deported to the United States in 1986.

5

AZERBAIJAN, ARMENIA, KARABAKH

ON DECEMBER 13, we flew back to Moscow, where we were met by three scholars from the Institute of Oriental Studies who had drafted a proposal for resolving the Armenian-Azerbaijanian conflict. That may be putting it a bit strongly, but their ideas were interesting, if controversial. Galina Starovoitova, an acquaintance of ours from the Institute of Ethnography, had come with them. Andrei Zubov served as spokesman for the group: he unrolled a map and explained the plan. The first step would be to conduct referendums in the regions of Azerbaijan with a high percentage of Armenians and in the regions of Armenia with a high percentage of Azerbaijanis, referendums posing the question: should this region be attached to Armenia or Azerbaijan? The project's authors assumed that approximately equal territories with approximately equal populations would switch from Armenia to Azerbaijan and vice versa. They hoped that the announcement of this scheme would turn people's minds from confrontation to dialogue and ultimately create a basis for more peaceful interethnic relations. Nonetheless, specially trained troops would have to be stationed in the troubled areas to ensure peace during the transition period. They expected that the Nagorno-Karabakh Autonomous Region (with the significant exception of the Shusha district, populated by Azerbaijanis) and the Shaumian region would leave Azerbaijan for Armenia.

The plan was worth discussing. The next day I phoned Alexander Yakovlev, told him my reason for calling, and asked for a meeting. A few hours later in Yakovlev's office I handed him a brief résumé (which I'd prepared the night before) of the verbose and rather pedantic draft proposal. Yakovlev said that the material was interesting, but in the current state of ethnic relations the idea of a peaceful realignment of territory was completely impracticable. "Why don't you go to Baku and Yerevan, and see for yourself?"

The phone rang just then; Yakovlev picked it up and asked me to step out to his secretary's office. Ten or fifteen minutes later he invited me back in and said that he had been speaking with Mikhail Sergeyevich [Gorbachev], who also believed that territorial changes were out of the question at this time. Mikhail Sergeyevich had independently suggested that it would be useful for me to visit Baku and Yerevan. "You could take along someone from your People's Tribune [Yakovlev deliberately garbled the name of the Moscow Tribune] and one of the authors of the proposal."

I replied that I'd like to include my wife in the delegation and that I'd let him know the other names. If he would make the necessary arrangements, we could leave almost immediately.

"Of course, of course. I could tell from the postscript concerning the detention of the Karabakh Committee that you personally wrote the résumé."

The Karabakh Committee had been formed in Yerevan to support the Armenians in Nagorno-Karabakh, and it had gained enormous influence in Armenia. It organized huge rallies, and when the central authorities' pro-Azerbaijanian bias became clear, it called for strikes. In November, when the Armenians began expelling Azerbaijanis from Armenia in retaliation for the actions of Azerbaijan, the Karabakh Committee tried to prevent violence. When everything was in a state of confusion during the first hours after the December 7 earthquake, the Committee mobilized rescue efforts and assistance, for remote hamlets as well as for the larger towns.

The following story, told by one of my colleagues, is typical: His son was trying—together with many fellow students—to go to Armenia, but he was informed that too many volunteers had gone there as it was. (The same thing happened in Kharkov, Kiev, and other cities.) The students got in touch with members of the Karabakh Committee in Moscow, who enabled them to reach Armenia. My colleague's son helped dig three people out of the rubble in Spitak; he and his friends all complained that if assistance had been promptly and properly organized thousands more could have been saved.

Gorbachev's trip to the disaster area didn't go well. He was harangued by a desperate, grieving people with nothing left to lose. He may have hoped that the earthquake would at least dispose of the Karabakh issue, but that didn't happen. Unfortunately, Gorbachev's reaction was irritable—I would even call it childishly peevish—and not sufficiently sensitive to the tragic circumstances. He spoke impatiently about bearded men, but a beard in Armenia is a sign of mourning. As soon as Gorbachev departed, the members of the Karabakh Committee were arrested on December 10 at the Yerevan Writers Club, where they were collecting and packaging emergency supplies for devastated villages. The arrests outraged Armenians (even those who disagreed with the Karabakh Committee's program). The Moscow Tribune took up their defense. The newspapers at first reported that the reason for the arrests was the Committee's disruption of rescue work; thereafter various other pretexts were put forward.

To return to my conversation with Yakovlev: I tried to convince him that freeing the Committee was absolutely necessary to calm the people in Armenia. He replied that the affair was in the hands of the legal authorities and no one had the right to interfere. I then asked about the laws adopted in July 1988 restricting public demonstrations and granting additional powers to the special forces of the Ministry of the Interior, and he attempted to justify them. I asked Yakovlev what the rush had been to adopt a new electoral law and amend the Constitution.* The Moscow Tribune had proposed holding a referendum on four of the issues involved.

---

*A special session (November 29–December 1, 1988) of the Supreme Soviet amended the 1977 Constitution to create a new 2,250-member Congress of People's Deputies as the USSR's highest legislative body, and a subsidiary working parliament chosen from it, a revamped Supreme Soviet (composed of a 271-member Council of the Union and a 271-member Council of Nationalities). Deputies are elected for five-year terms in contested elections. The Council of Ministers, the highest executive and administrative organ of the USSR, is responsible to the Supreme Soviet. The chairman of the Supreme Soviet (Gorbachev) was designated the head of state, but in further amendments adopted in March 1990, a president, with expanded powers and directly elected by the people, has replaced the chairman of the Supreme Soviet in that role, and two new bodies—a Council of the Federation, composed of the chief officers of the Union Republics, and an appointed Presidential Council—have been established to advise him. See David Lane, *Soviet Society Under Perestroika* (Unwin Hyman, 1990, pp. 353–385) for the text of the USSR Constitution, with amendments through December 20, 1989.

Yakovlev's reaction to this was particularly interesting. He exclaimed, "We can't waste time on a referendum. If we don't hurry, we'll be crushed!" (He didn't explain by whom, but I assumed he had right-wing opponents of *perestroika* in mind.) He'd objected at first to certain details in the election laws, but he was now convinced that in the current circumstances of danger from the right and inadequate experience with democratic elections, Gorbachev's proposal was the only possible way to go. In the future, much will have to be changed and nothing prevents that. In particular, he mentioned a two-chamber system, direct elections of the President, and the principle "one man, one vote." At the conclusion of our conversation Yakovlev gave me a copy of a speech he'd delivered in Perm a few days earlier, which hadn't been published in the central newspapers. Apparently he wanted to persuade me that he was the most determined advocate of *perestroika* among the top leaders.

The group that we formed to visit Azerbaijan and Armenia consisted of Andrei Zubov; Galina Starovoitova and Leonid Batkin from the Moscow Tribune; and Lusia and myself. The meeting with Yakovlev had taken place on a Monday. On Tuesday our documents were ready and we received tickets from the Central Committee office. Within twenty-four hours we flew to Baku, where we were met by the president of the Azerbaijan Academy of Sciences and one of his vice-presidents, the director of the Physics Institute, as I recall. The Central Committee had arranged that in both Armenia and Azerbaijan I was received as a guest of their respective Academies and treated with excessive deference. A representative of the military command gave us passes to move around after curfew, which was already in effect by the time we left the airport and headed into town. The director of the Physics Institute, who was traveling in our car, explained, "It was quiet here for nine months, but in November things grew tense, and we had to declare an emergency and impose a curfew. The neighborhoods where Armenians live are guarded very carefully."

On the way to the hotel we were stopped a dozen times by patrols. The roadblocks consisted of two tanks or armored cars on either side of the road, twenty or thirty feet apart, and detachments of armed soldiers and officers, in helmets and bulletproof vests. The officers would approach, check our passes carefully, and then wave us on. The soldiers stood nearby in silence. All had tired Russian faces—it was strange to see so many blond young men in the Caucasus.

We were installed in a large hotel, obviously reserved for the elite: there were few other guests to be seen. We took all our meals at Academy expense in a recently redecorated dining room. The next day we met with representatives of the Azerbaijan Academy, the scientific community, and the intelligentsia. The session was depressing. One after another, scientists and writers spoke at length, some sentimentally, others aggressively, about the friendship of peoples and its value. They assured us that no real problem existed in Nagorno-Karabakh, that it had always been Azerbaijanian territory, that the issue was invented by Abel Aganbegian [an Armenian, and one of Gorbachev's chief economic advisers] and the journalist Zori Balayan and kept alive by extremists. Moreover, any past mistakes had been corrected after the July session of the Presidium of the Supreme Soviet: all that was needed for the restoration of complete peace was the imprisonment of Genrikh Pogosian, the recently elected first secretary of Nagorno-Karabakh.

The audience didn't want to listen to Batkin and Zubov when they spoke about holding a referendum. They were continually interrupted, and Academician Zia Buniatov was particularly belligerent. (Buniatov is a historian, a war veteran, and a Hero of the Soviet Union, known for his anti-Armenian statements; he published an article attacking Lusia and me after our visit.) In speaking of Sumgait, he tried to depict the pogrom there as a provocation initiated by Armenian extremists and black-market speculators seeking to exacerbate the situation. He emphasized the participation of some man with an Armenian surname. When he interrupted Batkin in an insulting manner, I called Buniatov to order, saying that we were equal members of a delegation sent by the Central Committee to assess the situation.

Lusia supported me energetically, and then Buniatov attacked her and Starovoitova, shouting that they had been brought here to take notes. "So sit and write, and don't talk." Lusia got mad and responded sharply, something along the lines of: "Shut up, I pulled hundreds like you out of the line of fire when I was a nurse during the war."

Buniatov paled. He'd been publicly insulted by a woman. I don't know how an Oriental man is expected to behave in such situations, but Buniatov turned around and stalked out of the room without a word. Later, in the smoking room, he said to Lusia in a more respectful manner, "You may be an Armenian, but you must understand that you're not right." Of course, that audience could hardly have been expected to show any sympathy for Zubov's project. In fact, they simply refused to recognize that a problem existed.

That same day we had an equally tense meeting with Azerbaijanian refugees from Armenia. We were taken to a large auditorium where several hundred Azerbaijanis, men and women who looked like peasants, were waiting. The speakers, who doubtless had been carefully screened, all told of the horrors of their expulsion, of beatings, burning, and looting. Several spoke hysterically, building up a dangerously charged atmosphere in the auditorium.

I remember a young woman who shouted that Armenians had chopped children into pieces and ended with a triumphant wail, "Allah has punished them!" (She meant the earthquake! We knew that it brought joy to many in Azerbaijan, that they allegedly celebrated the news in the Baku region with a holiday and fireworks.) We asked the speakers to recount only what they had personally witnessed, but it was hopeless—things kept heating up more and more. When we inquired if anyone in the audience wanted to return to Armenia, the response was unanimous: "No, we don't!"

We asked the speakers: What do you want? What are your immediate problems? Typical requests were compensation for homes and other abandoned property; replacement of lost documents; housing and jobs; assistance in tracing relatives. An elderly policeman asked our help in getting a pension for the thirty-five years he had worked in Armenia (he complained that he had been severely beaten). Many spoke of the participation of local Armenian police and Party workers in the expulsions and in the atrocities committed. On the whole, despite some obvious fabrications, we were left with the impression that a great tragedy had occurred.

That same day we met with Lieutenant General Tyagunov, the military commandant of Baku. Tyagunov didn't have much time for us, less than a half-hour, and he spent the best part of it on compliments to Starovoitova; after that, we spent another half-hour with his deputy for political affairs, who told us that there had been many excesses in Baku and in other parts of Azerbaijan before martial law was declared. We heard details of Azerbaijanian violence against Armenians as a counterbalance to the stories of the refugees. Things had settled down in Baku, but there still was much work to be done, and the officers and soldiers were tired of sleeping on alert. It was very tense during rallies which involved up to 500,000 people. The slogans were primarily anti-Armenian and nationalist, but there were also green Moslem banners, pan-Islamic slogans, and portraits of Khomeini, though only a few. We were shown a red Pioneer neckerchief that had been made into a head scarf with a picture of Khomeini embroidered on it.

In the evening two Azerbaijanis came to see us at the hotel. They had been described to us as representatives of the progressive wing of the Azerbaijanian intelligentsia and as future Party bigwigs. Our guests spoke enthusiastically of the November mass rallies in Baku (which had in fact lasted until December 5), about their excellent organization and their populist character: they were signs of a surge in Azerbaijanian nationalist sentiment. The demonstrators had been guarded by an inner ring of Afghan veterans in their uniforms and an outer ring of police. Several checkpoints were established, allowing people to come and go. Here and there on the square people slaughtered sheep in the Shiite manner, and pilaf was cooked over campfires. The slogans, according to our visitors, were in the main progressive—against corruption and the mafia, and for social justice. Their personal views on nationality problems differed from Buniatov's, but not as much as one might hope. In any case, they considered Nagorno-Karabakh traditional Azerbaijanian territory, and they praised the young women who threw themselves in front of tanks with the cry, "We'll die before we give up Karabakh!"

The next day, we met with Abdul-Rakhman Vezirov, the Party First Secretary, who monopolized the conversation, using his voice, facial expressions, and gestures in an Oriental-style performance. He boasted of his success in improving interethnic relations during the brief time he had been on the job, and claimed that the majority of refugees—Armenians and Azerbaijanis—wanted to return to their former homes. (This directly contradicted what they themselves had told us. In fact, the status of the refugees remains a critical problem.) We asked Vezirov for his thoughts on our project. His first reaction was negative—there aren't any problems, everything has been resolved, past mistakes are being corrected. Then he changed his tune and exclaimed: "Whether there's one idea or a thousand, we'll examine them all."

Toward the end of the meeting, Lusia said, "You speak of friendship with the Armenians. They've suffered a great national tragedy. Thousands of people lost relatives, their possessions. The very existence of the Armenian nation is threatened. Eastern people are famed for their generosity. Do something noble—give Karabakh to Armenia, a gift to a friend in need. The whole world will be awed by this act. It will be remembered for generations!"

Vezirov's expression betrayed his irritation. "Land isn't given," he said disdainfully. "It's conquered." (He may have added "by blood," but I'm not absolutely certain of that.)

When we requested Vezirov to set up a meeting for us with Nemat Panakhov, who had been arrested in connection with the demonstrations, he replied that arranging such meetings was not his responsibility. We also asked if we might go directly to Karabakh, but he insisted that flying there from Baku was not a good idea, that it would be better to go first to Yerevan.

Vezirov got tickets for us, and in short order we arrived in Yerevan, the Armenian capital. Formally, our program there was analogous to the one in Azerbaijan—meetings with the Academy of Sciences, refugees, and the First Secretary—but life in Yerevan was monopolized by the aftermath of the earthquake. Prime Minister Nikolai Ryzhkov had left just the day before; he'd headed a special government commission and created a good impression, although quite a few costly organizational and other mistakes had been made immediately after the earthquake.

The future of the Armenian nuclear power plant particularly concerned me. It was a major supplier of energy to Armenia and neighboring Georgia, and technical, seismological, economic, and even psychological issues were involved. After the earthquake, the Armenians were in a state of shock and panic, almost mass psychosis. The fear of a nuclear accident added to their stress, and it was essential to allay their anxiety.

In the lobby of our hotel, we ran into the seismologist Vladimir Keilis-Borok (I had met him in the course of discussions on the possibility of triggering an earthquake by detonating an underground nuclear charge). He was in a rush, but he briefed me on the seismological situation in northern Armenia, where one broad fault line intersects another in the vicinity of Spitak, and in southern Armenia, where another fault line runs close to the nuclear power plant and Yerevan. You have to be crazy to build a reactor in a place like that, but that's not the only lunacy perpetrated by the agency that was responsible for Chernobyl: they still haven't abandoned the idea of building a nuclear power plant in the Crimea.

I visited the office of Viktor Ambartsumian, president of the Armenian Academy of Sciences, to discuss the Armenian plant. Academicians Evgeny Velikhov and Nikolai Laverov participated in the conversation, and Lusia was there, too.

Velikhov said, "If the reactor is taken out of service, then the power plant in Razdan will become the main source of energy. But that's also in a seismologically active region and there's a possibility that an earthquake could destroy it."

Lusia asked, "How long would it take to restart the nuclear reactors in that case?" Velikhov and Laverov looked at her as if she were mad. But the question made sense. In emergencies you have to reassess the bounds of the possible, as Lusia knew from her wartime experiences.

Zubov's project received no support at a meeting at the Armenian Academy. The thought of handing over to Azerbaijan the Shusha region (the part of Karabakh populated by Azerbaijanis)—or, more precisely, leaving it within the borders of Azerbaijan—dismayed those present. The Armenians said that the tragic situation hadn't diminished the importance of regaining Artsakh (the Armenian name for Karabakh), but it was now out of the question to turn over any territory whatsoever to Azerbaijan. Only Ambartsumian spoke of the need to seek compromise. Everyone condemned the arrest of the Karabakh Committee, and urged their release in order to reduce tension. They spoke of the need to shut down the nuclear reactors and of the seismological danger in Yerevan.

After the meeting ended, I was taken to a back room to meet one of the active members of the Karabakh Committee, Rafael Kazarian, a physicist in his mid-sixties and a corresponding member of the Armenian Academy. He had been arrested with the rest of the Committee on December 10, but was released after he signed a promise not to leave Yerevan. (A few days after our conversation he was rearrested.) He told me about the Committee and its work. The Committee members were charged with wanting to seize power and replace the existing authorities. Kazarian asked: "How can anyone believe that people with interesting jobs that they've left temporarily for the sake of the nation would ever want to take power?"

Batkin and Starovoitova managed a secret meeting that evening with Karabakh leaders in the underground. It was a whole spy novel, with passwords, signs, and secret passages. Their impressions coincided with those I got from my conversation with Kazarian, but theirs were more detailed.

While Batkin and Starovoitova were absent, Zubov, Lusia, and I met with refugees. Their stories were horrifying, and their problems were similar to those of the Azerbaijanian refugees—housing, work (impossible to obtain without residency permits), abandoned apartments, lost documents, destroyed property. The Armenians' difficulties were compounded by the simultaneous flow of refugees from the earthquake area and also by the fact that most of them were urban dwellers. None wanted to return to Azerbaijan, to hatred and violence, to threats and real danger.

The following day I met alone with the First Secretary of Armenia, Suren Arutiunian. He didn't want to discuss Zubov's proposal for readjustment of borders, so we talked about the refugees. He insisted that some were prepared to return to their former homes, and I disputed that. Arutiunian also spoke about the difficulties of resettling the refugees in Armenia after the earthquake and about acts of violence in areas where Azerbaijanis had been living. In late November, when Armenian refugees began to arrive in great numbers, about twenty Azerbaijanis had been killed, and an entire family, including young children, had frozen to death trying to cross a mountain pass without warm clothing.

Present during our talk was Yuri Batalin, chairman of the State Construction Commission and a member of the government commission appointed to superintend reconstruction after the earthquake, and so I took the opportunity to raise the issue of the nuclear power plant. (I also phoned Academician Anatoly Alexandrov and told him that the reactors should be shut down, but I don't recall the date of our conversation.)

Around noon, I rejoined the rest of our party, and the five of us flew to Stepanakert, the capital of Nagorno-Karabakh, together with our friend Yuri Rost, a photojournalist from *Literaturnaya gazeta*, and Zori Balayan, an Armenian journalist.

We were met at the Stepanakert airfield by Genrikh Pogosian, First Secretary of Nagorno-Karabakh and the official the Azerbaijanian Academicians wanted to have arrested, a man of medium height with an animated tanned face. He drove us to the building of the Party committee, where we met with Arkady Volsky, the representative of the Central Committee. (In January 1989, he was appointed chairman of the Committee of Special Rule when Karabakh was placed under Moscow's direct control.) Volsky briefed us on the situation. He said, "Two major mistakes were made back in the 1920s—the creation of the Nakhichevan and Nagorno-Karabakh Autonomous Regions and their subordination to the jurisdiction of Azerbaijan. The Aliev mafia* that took control of Azerbaijan came out of Nakhichevan. Karabakh became an insoluble problem for the people living here."

He told us about clashes between Azerbaijanis and Armenians, about the blockade of Armenian regions, about difficulties with supply (the Armenians were even cut off from their usual sources of water in the Azerbaijanian Shusha region). Shusha, which at the turn of the century had been the third most important city in the Caucasus, had become a ghost town after the Armenians were kicked out in the summer of 1988.

We met with Armenians and Azerbaijanis in Stepanakert and Shusha respectively, and these gatherings resembled the earlier ones in Yerevan and Baku. Before driving to Shusha, Volsky asked Lusia and me if we were sure we wanted to make the trip. "Things are unsettled there." Naturally, we went.

Volsky got in the back seat of our car; an armed guard rode in front with the driver. Batkin and Zubov went in a second car, also with a guard. Volsky refused to take Starovoitova and Balayan because they were "notorious."

During the meeting in Shusha, Volsky deftly kept passions in check, sometimes reminding the Azerbaijanis that they were not without sin. (For instance, he recalled how an Armenian woman had been beaten with sticks by Azerbaijanian women. There was a horrible story of twelve-year-olds torturing a boy of another nationality with electric shocks, driving him to jump out the window of the hospital where they were all patients.)

At the very beginning, Lusia announced, "I want to tell you who I am. I'm the wife of Academician Sakharov. My mother was Jewish, my father Armenian." (There was a commotion in the hall. Later an Azerbaijanian woman told Lusia, "You're a brave woman.") Lusia also said,

---

*Geydar Aliev, a career KGB officer, was First Secretary of Azerbaijan from 1969 to 1982, when Yuri Andropov moved him to Moscow as a Deputy Prime Minister. He was fired from the Politburo in October 1987.

in reference to the story about the boys, "I don't even know who the real victims were—the boy they tortured or the boys who were the torturers. It's horrible when ethnic hatred is passed on to children and mutilates their souls."

A gang of agitated Azerbaijanis stood waiting for us outside the buildings as we were preparing to leave. Volsky got out of the car, and said a few words that apparently calmed them down.

We took a trip to Topkhana, where Armenians were supposedly destroying a sacred grove in order to build an ecologically harmful factory. This story was printed in Azerbaijanian newspapers and had exacerbated already tense relations in October and November 1988. When we got to Topkhana, we saw lovely hills with the dachas of Azerbaijanian bigwigs clustered off to our right. All these years the elite (including Academicians) had vacationed there. That was the sacred precinct for which they were prepared to fight to the death (not their own, of course). Right in front of us was a big hill, rather bare, where they were going to build a camp for the children of the workers of a small metalworking factory, situated far below in the valley. There was never talk of locating anything ecologically harmful in Topkhana or chopping down a nonexistent grove. The mountain air and extended vistas were magnificent.

Lusia suggested that it would make an ideal site for an all-Union or international center for asthmatic children, or else a rehabilitation center for young victims of the earthquake, along with sanatoriums for adults. This could be done with the international assistance that was so generously pouring into Armenia; the project would create jobs for Armenians and Azerbaijanis, improve the area's economy, and ease ethnic strife.

When we bade farewell to Volsky, he reiterated that the only solution was the introduction of a special form of administration and a war on the mafia. "The mafia," he said, "cuts across ethnic lines. They [i.e., the Armenian and Azerbaijanian mafias] easily find a common language." He added that the underground economy in Azerbaijan had a capital of 10 billion rubles, and in Armenia 14 billion. After Volsky left, his assistant volunteered that once the Karabakh Committee members were released from prison, they could help root out the mafia from Armenia's Party and state apparatus.

That evening, in the dormitory of a silk factory where we were staying, we met with the local leaders of Krunk ("stork" in Armenian, a symbol of longing for the homeland—Krunk in Karabakh is the equivalent of the Karabakh Committee in Armenia). At dinner they expressed great fear of the proposed special administration. The new governing committee would replace all existing Party and state structures, but it wasn't clear whether it could resist pressure from Azerbaijan. They opposed separation of Shusha from Karabakh.

The next morning we flew to Yerevan and then on to the earthquake zone by helicopter, a new experience for Lusia and me. These marvelous machines come straight from the pages of science fiction, but now we were heading toward reality and tragedy. Young volunteers loaded the helicopter with crates of food and warm clothing, and we then took off for Spitak. Streaks in the snow marked the fault lines as we flew over the disaster area.

Suddenly I saw a destroyed village. At first, from the air, it looked ordinary, but then I could make out half-demolished houses and outbuildings, covered with fresh snow, and logs strewn about like matchsticks. No human beings were visible at all.

We continued on to Spitak and circled over the collapsed remains of multistory structures. All that was left of the former blocks of buildings was piles of rubble, but the streets were mostly intact. Cranes were in operation in two or three places, and in some spots people were scrabbling in the ruins, but there were only very few; most of the ground beneath us seemed depopulated, a scene of death and desolation. The helicopter wheeled sharply toward the village where we were to deliver our cargo. Not far from Spitak we passed over a town that had been totally wiped out. "That," said Balayan, "was the epicenter of the earthquake. Eleven on the Richter scale. Twenty-five hundred people died there."

At last the helicopter landed on a snowy field about four hundred feet from the destroyed village. People were running toward us, waving their arms. The helicopter crew unloaded the crates right in the snow. About forty people stood in a huddle with several strong-looking men in the front rank. We talked with several women. In their village, as everywhere else, almost all the schoolchildren had been killed (the earthquake occurred five minutes before the recess bell), including the grandchildren of the women we were speaking to. It was impossible to live in the houses; people were sleeping in haystacks.

The crew finished unloading and stepped aside. Shouting and pushing, the people lunged for the crates. The scene turned ugly, some grabbing too much, others getting nothing. The women we had been talking with snatched up armfuls of warm blankets and ran with them to the village. Two men began throwing crates of food into a truck. We tried to shame them out of it and they reluctantly returned the crates, but someone handed them up again from the other side. A man opened a jar of baby food (hard to come by even in Moscow) and took a taste with his finger. He didn't like it and tossed the jar into the snow. We asked a man standing to one side, eyes red with tears, "You need some warm clothing. Why don't you take some?" "I buried my wife two days ago, I'm not going to get into a .fight." And he walked away. A woman with small children began cursing the bosses and Soviet rule. The heli-copter crew told us that scenes like this were repeated every day. "They're embarrassed to be too brazen with you around. Sometimes there are real brawls. There aren't any lists, no one knows who's still alive, who needs what. The authorities have lost their heads or run off, and they steal more than anyone else." When we were back in the air, Balayan, shocked by what he had seen, burst into tears.

In Spitak we landed in the outskirts of the town. Volunteer students from Moscow were clearing away the rubble. They were living next to the site in a trailer. About a hundred yards away soldiers were at work, digging deep trenches and then pulling bodies from under ruins. It was the seventeenth day after the catastrophe. Many corpses were still buried under the rubble; the majority had apparently died immediately, but others called out for several days before they fell silent—a horrible death. You could smell decaying flesh. The soldiers and some of the students wore gas masks.

While we were still in flight, we had seen bright spots of color scat-tered in the snow—children's dresses, mittens, scarves, and so on. The wind from our landing ruffled the pages in one of the notebooks, and we could make out an A given to a homework assignment, with the date: December 5, 1988. It was impossible to see it without tears. A few steps further along, there were dolls and other toys. We were told that almost all the children in the school and kindergarten had died. (Later, back in Yerevan, Lusia suggested that the children's clothes and notebooks should be gathered up and kept in a museum, not left to rot in the snow.) Lusia entered a tent where a man and his wife were living. The wife and their son had been saved by Georgians from a civil defense unit that arrived just hours after the earthquake under the command of a quick-thinking colonel. Their daughter had been killed, and the son was in Georgia for treatment. Everyone in Spitak—residents and rescuers alike—complained about the inadequate supplies of food and water. No one had been paid the promised emergency relief (fifty or one hundred rubles, I don't remember which).

When we returned to the Yerevan airport from Spitak, we were shocked by the poor handling of the donations coming in from all over the world. There was something immoral in the high-and-mighty attitude of officials in the face of disaster. . . .

The next day, before leaving for Moscow, Lusia and I met with the Deputy Chairman of the Council of Ministers of Armenia. We told him what we had seen in the countryside and in Spitak and suggested ways to improve the situation. In particular we urged that competent people be sent to the villages to compile lists of the needy and to distribute the aid—this would bring some order to the distribution of relief supplies, which were falling into the wrong hands or simply disappearing. The Deputy Chairman listened to us with attention, but I'm afraid that little of our advice was taken. Rost, who stayed on in Armenia, told us that after a shipment of tents arrived many were diverted to the black market, and the same thing happened with drugs and other supplies.

When we got back to Moscow, I immediately called Yakovlev and briefed him on our experiences. Everyone in our expedition turned in written reports, but I'm afraid the authorities weren't really interested. I asked to go again to Armenia with Lusia, for the express purpose of helping to organize aid. I made this offer to Ryzhkov, and he seemed prepared to send us there, but later on, perhaps at Gorbachev's behest, he changed his mind.

6

BEFORE THE CONGRESS

IN LATE DECEMBER I spoke at a General Assembly of the Academy of Sciences devoted to ecology and singled out the excessive power of central government agencies as the principal reason for the disastrous ecological situation in our country. I named such organizations as the Ministry of Water Resources, the Ministry of Energy, and the Ministry of the Timber and Paper Industry. I spoke of the responsibility of the Academy to take an objective, scientifically based stand in favor of environmental protection instead of serving as a complacent adjunct of the state bureaucracy. Providing independent ecological expertise for major projects and state planning should become a priority for the Academy. I spoke about two specific problems: the Armenian nuclear plant and the Volga-Chograi Canal.

I've already written about the first problem. Quite soon thereafter, a special commission ordered the shutdown of the Armenian reactors, and I like to think that my intervention had something to do with this. In any case, during a break at the General Assembly, Anatoly Alexandrov came over and said that he had passed along my recommendation even though he disagreed with me.

As for the construction of the Volga-Chograi Canal, the whole idea is ridiculous from an economic point of view. It will cost four billion rubles—enough to build grain elevators, roads, and a lot of other things that would far outweigh any possible benefits from the canal. Besides, there is no great shortage of water in the Stavropol region. The canal would, moreover, be extremely harmful ecologically; it might well cause serious oversalinity in the Kalmyk region, the diversion of water from the Volga would finish off the osetra sturgeon and might make it necessary to change the course of northern rivers, a project that is still being pushed by the Ministry of Water Resources even though it has been canceled because of the damage it would do the environment.

The Volga-Chograi Canal was discussed by the Academy Presidium. Not trusting the Academy's bureaucracy, four academicians (Alexei Yablokov, Nikolai Vorontsov, Alexander Yanshin, and I) sent a telegram to Gorbachev and Ryzhkov explaining our point of view.

IN EARLY JANUARY 1989 (on the 6th, I believe) Gorbachev invited members of the intelligentsia—famous writers, scientists, and artists—to meet with him. There had been similar gatherings before, but this was the first time I had been invited. Ryzhkov was present, but did not speak. The meeting began with Gorbachev's rather long-winded opening remarks. *Perestroika,* he declared, was entering its decisive phase and prompt action was called for; at the same time, excessive haste should be avoided and necessary intermediate steps should not be skipped. The danger from the right and the danger from the left are equally serious. It is important to consolidate all the constructive forces in the country, to unite them around the basic principles of *perestroika,* to recognize that disagreements on specifics are permissible and even healthy so long as they don't lead to squabbling and personal hostility.

Gorbachev seemed to be trying to make peace among the various writers' groups and other cultural cliques. But it was clear from the first speeches made by writers of the Russophile wing and their ideological opponents that differences had gone too far to be so simply resolved. The speakers didn't limit themselves to culture; they discussed economic, social, ethnic, and legal issues as well. A summary of the speeches was published, but the more biting remarks, both political and personal, were omitted.

I had planned to speak, but hesitated, not quite sure what to say. When I did make up my mind, the list was too long and I was unable to get the floor.

Academician Leonid Abalkin painted a vivid picture of the economic crisis and summed up: "The cavalry charge against the administrative-command system failed, and we must switch to siege tactics." He had said pretty much the same thing at the Nineteenth Party Conference. I thought that Abalkin's position was too radical for Gorbachev, but a few months later I saw that I was wrong. [In June 1989, Abalkin was appointed Deputy Prime Minister for economic affairs.]

The writer Viktor Astafiev complained that the new laws on public meetings and on the powers of the special forces were antidemocratic and could be construed in a way that would preclude peaceful demonstrations; that had already happened in Minsk, in Kuropaty, in Krasnoyarsk, and other places. Gorbachev began arguing with Astafiev, using the pogrom in Sumgait as evidence for the need to be able to react quickly to events. "We were three hours late in Sumgait, and there was a tragedy. The workers insist that we prevent anarchy."

It was clear to me that Gorbachev was lumping together two completely different things—criminal acts of violence in Sumgait and constitutional, peaceful public meetings. It's a mistake to fear a democratic movement from below; without it, *perestroika* is impossible. The reference to workers had obviously been invented on the spur of the moment. I started making my way toward the podium from my seat, which was in the last row, hoping to get the floor. But when I heard Gorbachev say, "We were three hours late in Sumgait," I couldn't help myself and shouted out, "Not three hours, three days. There was a battalion of troops at the bus depot, but they didn't receive any orders. It's only a half-hour's drive to Baku. . . ."

Gorbachev, angered by my interruption, retorted, "You've been listening to demagogues" (it was clear that he meant Armenians, but he later softened his comments a bit). I handed in a request to speak, hoping to talk about the new laws and about the Memorial Society, but my name wasn't called.

During a break, I went over to Gorbachev and Ryzhkov and warned them that forcing Armenian and Azerbaijanian refugees to go back to their previous homes would lead to new tragedies. I also urged the release of the Karabakh Committee. Gorbachev listened with irritation, and Ryzhkov, it seemed to me, with interest. But it was the latter who rebuffed me, referring, like Yakovlev, to the impossibility of interfering with a criminal investigation in progress. Ryzhkov also said that he could not take me with him to Armenia because it would provoke the Azerbaijanis (we were talking about organizing relief assistance). Ryzhkov said that he'd received our telegram opposing the Volga-Chograi Canal. He hadn't known that the cost of construction would be four billion rubles, he'd thought it would be only half that. I noted that if they were really going to prevent seepage from the canal—an absolute necessity from the ecological point of view—then the cost would exceed four billion rubles. The whole conversation with Ryzhkov was very friendly.

IN THE SUMMER and fall of 1988, I refused a number of nominations to the Supreme Soviet (this was before the Constitution was amended in December 1988 to make the Congress of People's Deputies the supreme legislative body). Later, in January, after my candidacy for the Congress was supported by large majorities in many Academy institutes, I decided that I couldn't refuse, especially since I hoped that as a deputy I would be able to promote progressive initiatives in a more effective way. I don't remember the exact date when I agreed to run, because at the time I was convinced that the whole affair would end with my nomination, and that I wouldn't be permitted to run in the actual elections. I was right in a way, but I failed to foresee all the turns events would take.

The electoral law adopted in December 1988 is complex, but knowledge of its key provisions is necessary for an understanding of subsequent events. Of the Congress's 2,250 deputies, a third, or 750, were elected from territorial districts based on population; another 750 from territorial districts based on the formula of 32 from each Union Republic, 11 from each Autonomous Republic, 5 from each Autonomous Region, and one from each Autonomous District; and the final 750 from so-called public organizations, including the Communist Party (100 seats) and the Academy of Sciences (30 seats).

Candidates are formally nominated by meetings of work collectives, but the law as written requires their confirmation by regional committees or by the central organs of public organizations. This provision favors reactionaries, since the Party *apparat* and local bureaucrats can eliminate "unsuitable" candidates. Luckily, they didn't always manage to do so, but it's nonetheless essential to repeal this obstacle to free nominations.

The law doesn't make clear the precise manner in which the central organs of a public organization should elect deputies. The Presidium of the Academy decided that the process should be managed by a body, the Plenum, consisting of the members of the Presidium and of the governing boards of the Academy's [eighteen] departments. On January 18 the

Plenum was supposed to nominate a list of candidates for the Congress, and the Presidium decided that all Academicians and Corresponding Members (close to 900 persons) and about 550 electors (one for every sixty staff members at the Academy's affiliated institutes) would be eligible to vote in the election scheduled for March 21. Twenty-five instead of thirty seats were to be filled, since five places had been turned over to particular scientific societies.

The result was astonishing: at the first meeting of the Plenum all the popular candidates, including myself (I had been nominated by almost sixty institutes), Roald Sagdeyev, Dmitri Likhachev, and Gavriil Popov, failed to receive the required majority of votes; only twenty-three persons passed this hurdle. The Plenum then decided to transfer five more seats to scientific societies, leaving only twenty for the Academy itself. These manipulations stirred up a storm of protest at the institutes. The rank-and-file scientists who did real research justly felt that the Plenum had disregarded its mandate (according to the law, the Plenum must "take into account" the opinion of the working collectives), and they complained about the general bureaucratic alienation of the Academy's leaders and its Presidium. The public activity sparked by the phony nominating process soon grew beyond the immediate point at issue, as so often happens. An Initiative Group was formed by the Moscow institutes to coordinate activity relating to the Academy elections, and Anatoly Shabad and A. A. Sobyanin from FIAN became members.

Similar confrontations took place in other public organizations and in most election districts. Besides *apparatchiki* themselves and their tame stand-ins, alternative candidates, running on independent platforms, were nominated almost everywhere. For the first time in many years, real election contests developed in our country. And something happened that not even those of us who had led a circumscribed, lonely, and apparently hopeless struggle for civil rights in the Brezhnev era had anticipated. The people, deceived so often, surrounded by hypocrisy, corruption, crime, influence-peddling, and inertia, turned out to be alive and kicking. The possibility for change was still only a glimmer, but hope and the will for political action grew in people's hearts, and their enthusiasm made possible the emergence of the bold and independent new deputies we saw at the Congress. God help us if their expectations are frustrated—historically, there is never a last chance, but psychologically, for our generation, the disappointment might prove to be irreparable.

Of course, only a few of the progressive candidates made it to the Congress. The *apparatchiki,* bouncing back from the unexpected reverses of the first few weeks, began using all the means at their command, including forgery, stuffed ballot boxes, and their monopoly of the media, in order to install their "placemen." But this at least had the effect of ensuring that those who did triumph against official opposition were tempered fighters.

After January 18, I and several others who had been rebuffed by the Academy were nominated in various territorial electoral districts. FIAN nominated me in Moscow's October District, and my candidacy was supported by other institutes located there. I spoke before an election meeting at FIAN and then at the Party district committee, where I met the other candidates for the October District seat, including the eventual victor, Ilya Zaslavsky, whose platform included a plank for the rights of the disabled (he himself was left handicapped by a childhood illness). Before the FIAN meeting, I drafted my campaign program, and then I kept fine-tuning it.

I was nominated by Memorial and by many other enterprises and organizations for National District Number 1, the city of Moscow. I spoke at a meeting organized by Memorial at Dom Kino, the House of Cinematographers. As I drove up, I saw a line of people extending for several hundred yards. They were a familiar-looking crowd—the kind of people you see waiting to get into a Chagall exhibition or a film festival: honest and intelligent, understanding everything, the impoverished proletariat of mental labor.

New characters were appearing on the stage of history. Just a few months later, they would fill the gigantic field next to Luzhniki Stadium. Blue-collar and white-collar workers, the masses of the intelligentsia, had been roused from passivity by *perestroika.*

As I entered the Dom Kino, I was greeted with enthusiasm. Lev Ponomarev introduced me at the meeting, I read my program, and then replied to many questions, some quite difficult. Six hundred people in the hall and several thousand more outside (loudspeakers had been set up) signed nomination petitions for me.

That day, I felt that I had received a moral mandate to serve as a deputy. The second time I felt that way was on February 2 at a rally of Academy institutes. But even before that, I spoke at Moscow University, and received its nomination for District Number 1. At the same time,

Anatoly Logunov, the rector, was also nominated. Altogether, about ten people were nominated for the first district, including Boris Yeltsin, who called me at this time to suggest that we stay out of each other's way. I agreed, but added that I would make my final decision only after the regional meetings in the districts where I was nominated. A few days later, on Ponomarev's advice, I called Yeltsin and said that I was prepared to support him in the district where he would run if he would support me in mine. That smacked too much of backroom politics, and I soon came to regret it; fortunately, as it turned out, it had no practical consequences. I was nominated in four other Moscow districts, in one Leningrad district, in Kamchatka, in the Kola Peninsula, and in quite a few other places. I was also nominated at the Installation; my former colleague Viktor Adamsky and other activists visited me to get a copy of my program and some biographical details. They assured me that my nomination was practically a sure thing, but it didn't seem right to be elected for my work on nuclear weapons, or to exploit my reputation in that world.

On February 2 there was an unprecedented meeting of scientists from the Academy's institutes. The rally was organized by the Initiative Group for Elections which I've mentioned earlier, and permission was granted by the Moscow City Council to gather in the large square facing the mansion that houses the Academy's Presidium. Some three thousand people turned up (other estimates put the figure at more than five thousand). Microphones were set up on the steps of the building. President Guri Marchuk, Vladimir Kotelnikov, chairman of the Academy's Election Commission, and several other Academicians peeked out occasionally from behind a curtain on the second floor. Lusia and I arrived in an Academy car. I stood in the front ranks, near the tribunal, but I didn't speak.

The purpose of the rally was to express the scientific community's opposition to the Plenum's nominating procedures of January 18 and to the views of the Presidium and the Academy leadership in general. The institutes came in entire columns, carrying banners with appropriate slogans. You could sense the excitement of thousands of people who had cast off their chains and suddenly realized that they were a powerful force, that they should and could correct an intolerable situation.

At the start of the rally, Anatoly Shabad read the slogans aloud and the crowd echoed him.

"Worthy deputies for the Congress!"

"Shame on the Presidium bureaucrats!"

"Sakharov, Sagdeyev, Popov, Shmelyov—to the Congress!"

"The Presidium should resign!"

"The President should resign!"

"The Academy needs a decent President!"

At first, the meeting decided to boycott the elections on March 21, but then a resolution was passed to vote against the entire slate of candidates in order to force a repetition of the whole electoral process. After the rally, Lusia said, "I was certain you'd announce that you wanted to be nominated by the Academy and would turn down all other nominations."

I replied, "I understand the importance of the struggle in the Academy, and I want to support the resolution. [In the press and elsewhere, people were saying, "What difference does it make that Sakharov and Sagdeyev aren't on the Academy list, since they've been nominated elsewhere?"] But I also feel a responsibility to those who've nominated me and are supporting me in the election districts. That's why it's hard for me to do what you suggest."

I vacillated a few more days, even sending our Canadian hosts into a panic (we were supposed to travel there in February) by warning them that I might remain in Moscow to participate in the election campaign. Shabad, Fainberg, Fradkin, Ponomarev, and all my other supporters at FIAN asked me not to rule out the possibility of running from one of the election districts. Just one day before our departure for the West I finally wrote a letter to *Moscow News* [no. 8, 1989], announcing that I wouldn't "run for election anywhere else except the USSR Academy of Sciences. . . . I am profoundly grateful to all collectives and citizens who nominated me [and ask them to] understand that my decision is intended to support the will of the Academy's research workers."

ON FEBRUARY 5 I left for my second trip abroad, this time accompanied by Lusia. We flew first to Rome, where I met with many political figures, including Alessandro Pertini, the former President of Italy and a staunch supporter of Lusia and me, and Bettino Craxi, the president of the Italian Socialist Party. I visited the famous Accademia dei Lincei, where my diploma as a foreign member had long been waiting for me. One of the oldest academies in the world, its name reflects the move away from the stultifying scholasticism of the Middle Ages to the experimental study of nature. The lynx (*lince* in Italian) has a keen eye and a thirst for exploration and discovery.

The highlight of our brief stay in Rome was our meeting with the Pope. Lusia had met him in December 1985, when she asked for his help in ending my exile in Gorky. She had been touched by the humanity and responsiveness of the man. Now that our personal affairs were in much better shape, we spoke with the Pope about the complexities and contradictions of Soviet life, and I tried to formulate the basic principles of a sensible policy toward the USSR and *perestroika*. I speak of these same matters whenever I meet with government officials or appear in public, but in my conversation with the Pope I felt his exceptional and genuine interest and a deep intuitive understanding.

The visit to the Vatican made a great impression on me. Father Sergio Mercanzin escorted us through the magnificent gardens and palace, and Irina Alberti interpreted during my conversation with the Pope. Irina's role was enormous in our meetings in Italy: she translated my not always simple or smooth speech eloquently and wisely, sometimes improving on the original. Having suffered with numerous translators who didn't know Russian well, I particularly appreciated Irina's skill. And, of course, she was a friend, who shared our concerns.

After seeing the Pope, we met with Cardinal Lubachivsky of the Ukrainian Catholic (Uniate) church and then left for Florence. On the way I managed to see the Basilica of St. Francis in Assisi and Giotto's frescoes. It was after visiting hours, but the monk on duty recognized me; he called his superiors and the doors of the church were opened.

We stayed in Florence at the home of Lusia's friend Nina Harkevich. From there, we made day trips by car to Bologna and Siena, where I was awarded honorary degrees. These ceremonies in ancient universities (the one in Bologna is the oldest in the world) were unforgettable, with solemn processions of faculties dressed in medieval robes, with heralds and maces, with ancient music and lofty rhetoric. At every step in Italy you come into contact with history, with the sources of our civilization— Russians are, after all is said and done, Europeans.

In Rome we saw the Forum, the Colosseum ("Stormy Rome rejoices, the broad arena applauds triumphantly . . .").* You can't be proud of everything, but this was part of the past, although it seems disconnected from the present. We heard how centuries ago Siena's city council lived and worked in the *questura,* running the city's affairs, but the screams of the criminals executed daily in the adjacent square interfered with the sleep of the city fathers—so they moved the place of execution elsewhere. It never occurred to them that the rack should be abolished entirely, or that there should be fewer executions.

JUMPING AHEAD somewhat, on May 14 I made a second brief trip to Italy for the annual convention of the Italian Socialist Party. Irina Alberti had called and asked us to come if possible—just being present at the Congress and saying a few words in support of Bettino Craxi would be enough. We left Moscow at 7 P.M. and spent the night in a hotel in Milan. In the morning, after the inevitable TV interview, we were taken to the convention site and to the trailer that served as headquarters for Craxi and his staff. Through the thin wall we could hear speakers, applause, singing that reminded us of the revolutionary hymns and the May Day parades of our childhood. Delegates kept passing through the trailer, very much at ease. After a half hour, Craxi arrived, and together we entered the factory building that served as an auditorium, receiving an ovation as we mounted the tribune. Craxi introduced me. I said that my wife and I had come out of friendship and gratitude to the Socialist Party and to Bettino Craxi, who had helped us so much in our difficult times. "Other parties and leaders did a great deal, but you did the most."

Then I spoke of the situation in the USSR, the goals of the Congress, and the role of the outside world in support of *perestroika.* I was handed a bouquet of carnations. I raised it over my head and exclaimed, "The carnation is the symbol of workers' unity! For peace! For your freedom and ours!"

Irina, as usual, translated brilliantly. She said that Craxi had been beaming throughout my speech. Immediately after it was over, we headed for the airport and took off for Frankfurt in a small private plane,

*The opening lines of Mikhail Lermontov's "The Dying Gladiator" (1836).

which belonged to a businessman, a staunch supporter of the Socialist Party. Irina, Lusia, and I sat in the comfortable seats, watching a tiny plane creeping along the map of Italy, Switzerland, and Germany on a color monitor. In Frankfurt we said goodbye to Irina and took an Aeroflot flight that got us back to Moscow that evening. There was a long line for taxis, and we had to pay a gypsy cab in dollars—no one wanted rubles, another sign of the times.

Now, BACK TO our February trip. From Italy we flew to Canada, a completely different world—a prosperous, hard-working nation, not smug in any way, not self-centered, without very much in the way of history. Canada could serve as a model country, I remarked in one of my speeches, if it weren't so difficult to follow the example of others.

In Ottawa we were given honorary doctorates. (There is a photograph of the two of us in our gowns; Lusia is receiving her cap with a tassel.) In her response, Lusia mentioned the bilingual tradition of Ottawa University—English and French enjoy equal status there—as a sensible attempt to deal with the language question, a difficult problem in the Soviet Union as well.

At a press conference in Ottawa I was asked by a Novosti Press correspondent: "Tomorrow you'll meet with the Prime Minister and the Minister of Foreign Affairs. Are you planning to seek their help in freeing our boys who are being held prisoner in Afghanistan and Pakistan?"

I replied, "The release of prisoners of war is not Canada's affair. Only the recognition of the mujahideen by their opponents and direct negotiations about an exchange of prisoners—after all, there are mujahideen POWs held in Kabul and Tashkent—can gain the release of our Soviet POWs! Our country waged a cruel and horrible war in Afghanistan. We call our enemies bandits and don't recognize them as the armed forces of a belligerent. But bandits don't have prisoners of war, they have hostages. There have been reports that our helicopters have shot surrounded Soviet soldiers to prevent their being taken prisoner."

My last sentence was printed in *Krasnaya zvezda*, the official newspaper of the Ministry of Defense, and elsewhere in the USSR, and it provoked angry protests from top Soviet officers, from soldiers who had served in Afghanistan, and from ordinary readers. They described acts of heroism by Soviet helicopter pilots who risked their lives to save surrounded comrades (which in itself does not disprove the occurrence of incidents of the sort I'd mentioned). I had allegedly insulted the Soviet army, the memory of Soviet soldiers who died performing their international duty. These charges against me were repeated during the elections and at the Congress.

The Western press in Ottawa didn't report the episode at all. They were much more interested in Lusia's remarks about Jewish émigrés from the USSR. In replying to a question, she observed, "There's a tendency to regard all Jews leaving the USSR as political refugees. That isn't right or fair. We've always fought for the right of *everyone* to leave any country and to return to their own country. But many Jewish émigrés, and particularly those who choose to settle in the U.S. or Canada rather than Israel, are not motivated by political considerations. People can have other, fully legitimate reasons for leaving the USSR—a desire to live well, to realize their potential. But why do such people have a better right to call themselves political refugees and to get special privileges than refugees from Vietnam, Cambodia, or Armenia?"

Lusia's pronouncement caused a furor when it appeared in the Canadian press. She was accused of anti-Semitism and other mortal sins. We were warned that outraged Jews would picket our appearances in Winnipeg, where I was invited to a seminar on magnetic resonance scanning. But no such demonstrations occurred.

At a dinner in our honor given in a luxurious private home in Winnipeg, I got to talking with the violinist, an elderly Jew from Odessa, who had taught at Stolyarsky's famous school and played in a major orchestra. He had emigrated many years before and ended up in Canada. For a long time he was unemployed. "They don't have our musical culture or tradition. I was lucky to find a job as a music teacher at a public school," he said bitterly. Lusia and I felt uncomfortable sitting at the head table while the performers—the violinist and an accordionist—were standing a few steps from us. (It's different in a restaurant, I don't know why.)

We spent the second half of our trip privately with our children and grandchildren in the U.S. I had a chance to take a look at the English translation of my *Memoirs* and correct a number of inaccuracies. Lusia and I spent five wonderful days with all four grandchildren on Amelia Island, a Florida resort. We even saw an alligator in the wild.

Lusia stayed on after my departure in order to spend another month with the children and grandchildren in Massachusetts and to work intensively on the book about her childhood. In Moscow, especially when I'm around, she doesn't have a minute for herself, even for routine things.

ON MARCH 18 I returned to the USSR to take part in the Academy elections. The first day was devoted to discussion of the procedures and the candidates. The second day was for the elections themselves and tallying the votes. Members of the Initiative Group for Elections who were monitoring the proceedings noted that one of the vote counters reported a suspiciously large number of votes in favor of the candidates, and they also remarked that the individual concerned kept his briefcase on the table alongside the ballots (which violated all the rules, of course). When these matters were reported to Vladimir Kotelnikov, chairman of the Election Commission, he said that deviations from the mean happen and should cause no surprise.

That same evening, the unofficial tally showed that eight candidates had got the minimum 50 percent of the votes cast needed for election as deputies, but fifteen had failed to receive a majority, thus leaving twelve seats unfilled. (Perhaps one or two of the eight victorious deputies owe their election to the suspect briefcase.)

The next day the official results were announced, and new elections were scheduled for April 13. The institutes began a new cycle of nominations, and the Initiative Group compiled a list of candidates receiving support from multiple institutes (more than one, more than ten, more than twenty, and so on), and submitted the list to the Presidium. This time I was supported by almost all of the Academy's affiliates— more than two hundred in all. The Presidium tried to regain control of the situation, issuing new regulations for nominating "electors" from the institutes and reducing their numbers, but this no longer had any real significance. The Plenum once again served as an obedient tool in the hands of the Academy's president, Guri Marchuk, confirming the candidates he proposed and rejecting the nominees proposed by me and other participants in the Plenum's deliberations. But Marchuk didn't want another battle, and he followed most of the Initiative Group's recommendations (although with a few particular, and regrettable, exceptions).

On April 12 or 13 a General Assembly of the Academy discussed the nominations endorsed by the Plenum. The candidates presented their programs and answered questions; the discussion was heated at times.

A group of young people stood at the entrance to Moscow University soliciting votes against Academician Georgy Arbatov, director of the Institute of the U.S.A. and Canada.* Yuri Karyakin spoke in his behalf, saying that in the past, when Arbatov enjoyed the trust of the government, he had helped people who were falsely accused. He claimed that those who were on the street calling for votes against Arbatov were members of Pamyat [a right-wing Russian nationalist society].

Sagdeyev also spoke, describing Arbatov's activities in the corridors of power as progressive and useful, for which Arbatov had been obliged to pay by publicly supporting the official line. (Sagdeyev had told me the same thing a few days earlier when I questioned his support for Arbatov.)

Arbatov was asked if it was true that he had recently fired several scholars at his institute and, as a follow-up, whether one of those fired wasn't the same Yakovlev who had attacked Sakharov in print? Arbatov replied, "Yes, he's the one."

Unfortunately, I abstained from this discussion, I wasn't sure what to do. In retrospect, this all strikes me as having followed a well-rehearsed script. My reluctance to impugn Sagdeyev's position deterred me from speaking out against Arbatov.

There was another incident, directly involving my candidacy. After many speakers had praised me, Academician Valentin Koptyug, a member of the Presidium, came to the rostrum and said, "I'm often asked if I voted against Sakharov at the January 18 Plenum. I've nothing to hide, I voted against him, and I'll explain why. I admire Academician Sakharov for his scientific achievements. But some points in his campaign program seemed to me mistaken and dangerous. He wrote about a free market for labor, which would in fact involve the creation of a reserve army of unemployed, and that would have severe social repercussions. Sakharov also proposed making the lands of unprofitable collective farms immediately available for private lease. The unreality of this de-

---

*Arbatov is generally identified with the liberal wing of the establishment intelligentsia, and some reformers found a haven in his institute during the Brezhnev years; but in the opinion of many, his statements during that period defending Soviet actions— among them, the exile of Sakharov—went beyond the bounds of decency.

Sakharov with Elena Bonner and his stepson, Alexei Semyonov, Moscow, January 1987.

LEFT: Press conference of the Forum for a Nuclear-Free World, Moscow, February 15, 1987. BELOW: With Prime Minister Margaret Thatcher at the British Embassy, Moscow, March 31, 1987.

With the grandchildren, Anya and Matvei Yankelevich, at Sheremetevo
Airport, Moscow, June 2, 1987.

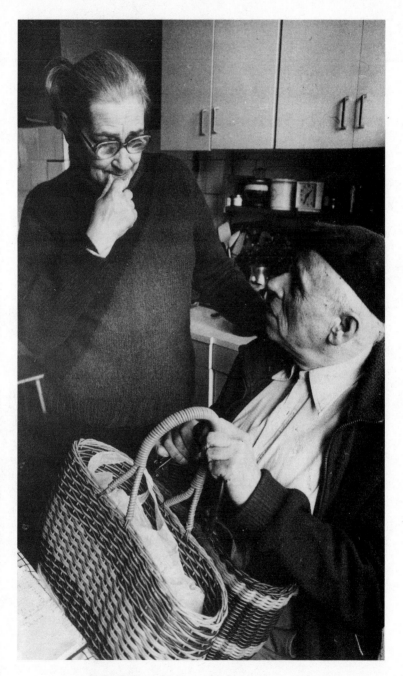

In the Sakharov's Moscow kitchen, autumn, 1987.

ABOVE: Last photo of Ruth Bonner, Moscow, December 20, 1987. OPPOSITE PAGE, ABOVE: Sergei Kovalev and Larisa Bogoraz working with the Sakharovs to prepare a statement on prisoners of conscience to be sent to Mikhail Gorbachev, January 14, 1988. RIGHT: At the birth of the "Moscow Tribune," Protvino, near Moscow, August 1988. *Left to right:* Leonid Batkin, Len Karpinsky, Gennady Zhavoronkov, Yuri Karyakin, Sakharov, Bonner, Yuri Afanasiev.

At the New York Academy of Sciences, November 1988. At far left, the American mathematician Joel Lebowitz; second from right, Sergei Kovalev.

With Edward Teller, Washington, D.C., November 1988.

ABOVE: With Ronald Reagan at the White House, November 1988. OPPOSITE PAGE, ABOVE: With Tatyana Yankelevich in Newton, Massachusetts, November 1988. OPPOSITE PAGE, BELOW: With members of the group Scientists for Sakharov, Orlov, Shcharansky, in Newton, Massachusetts, December 1, 1988. Standing (left to right): Robert Kahn, Morris Pripstein, Sakharov, Philip Siegelman, William Wentzel; seated: Kurt Gottfried.

ABOVE: With the mayor of Florence, Italy, February 10, 1989. OPPOSITE PAGE:
In Spitak, the epicenter of the Armenian earthquake of December 1988.
At right is the helicopter pilot who brought the Sakharovs to the site.

Sakharov supporting the campaign of Revolt Pimenov (at right) for People's Deputy, Syktyvkar, Komi Autonomous SSR, May 19, 1989.

The Sakharovs in May 1989. (Jean-Claude Bouis)

Sakharov in his living room, May 1989. (Jean-Claude Bouis)

Addressing the first Congress of People's Deputies, June 1989.
Mikhail Gorbachev is in the background.

mand is obvious. Sowing has already begun. This is extremism. Later Sakharov changed his views on these points, thereby admitting his error. But those suggestions were in his original platform." (I've used quotation marks here and in a number of other places in this book even though I can't vouch for the accuracy of every word.)

One of the subsequent speakers said, "We must be grateful to Academician Koptyug for his speech. Votes will almost certainly be cast against Sakharov, and if he received only praise, it would be difficult to account for the negative ballots."

I subsequently realized that the reason Koptyug gave for his vote against me at the January 18 Plenum was false. I still hadn't committed my program to writing by January 18; I did so only a few days later for the meeting at FIAN.

The balloting was conducted the next day. I was elected, but not with the highest number of votes by any means—I ranked somewhere in the middle among the twelve successful candidates. Arbatov squeaked through, almost at the end of the list. In general, those elected were capable, energetic people.

After the elections, the Initiative Group continued to function in a new role, offering administrative assistance to the new deputies from the Academy, helping them get in touch with their counterparts from other regions of the country, drafting and circulating a letter that could serve as a platform for an association of progressive deputies. While the Congress was in session, representatives of the Initiative Group were constantly on duty at the House of Scientists, where delegates frequently caucused.

In late March, even before the second round of Academy elections, a group of twenty or thirty deputies from Moscow city and Moscow region began meeting at the House of Political Enlightenment on Trubnaya Square. After some hesitation, I joined the group. It included several radical economists (Gavriil Popov, Nikolai Shmelyov, Alexei Emelyanov, Vladimir Tikhonov, Nikolai Petrakov, and others) who were preparing briefing papers on the economic and social reforms needed to avert the imminent economic crisis. Other deputies worked on a draft agenda, rules of procedure, and additional materials for the Congress. I took part in these discussions and wrote a statement setting forth the need for the Congress to assume all legislative power and another one summarizing my ideas on the nationality question.

* * *

IN THIS CONNECTION, it is important to recall the events in Georgia that cast a shadow over the Congress. In the spring of 1989, Georgians demonstrated in Tbilisi on several occasions to protest Abkhazian demands for the transfer of jurisdiction over the Abkhazian Autonomous Republic from Georgia to the Russian Republic. Abkhazians are a minority in their Autonomous Republic because of "Georgification," or so they claim. Thousands of Abkhazians displayed their dissatisfaction with the existing state of affairs at a rally in Lykhny, the ancient center of Abkhazia. But the majority of Georgians reject any possibility of change in their frontiers for economic reasons, and out of concern for the fate of the Georgian majority in Abkhazia.

I am on the whole more sympathetic to the Abkhazian position: the freedoms and rights of larger nations shouldn't be bought at the expense of smaller ones, which are entitled to special consideration. But the immediate point I want to make is that the demonstrations in Tbilisi, despite their peaceful and constitutional character, were crushed with extraordinary ferocity, and this was done at a time when the Tbilisi demonstrations seemingly had shifted their focus from the Abkhazian issue to the more general question of "sovereignty" in the sense of cultural and economic autonomy, not in the sense of secession from the USSR. But even calls for secession are sanctioned by the Constitution. . . .

On the morning of April 8, newly arrived military units, dressed in battle fatigues, paraded through the streets of Tbilisi with tanks. This show of force, probably intended to intimidate the Georgians, produced a contrary effect: that night more than ten thousand people gathered in Tbilisi's main square—most evenings, less than a thousand had been turning out for the protest meetings. At 4 A.M. on April 9, troops attacked the crowd. People were beaten over the head with entrenchment tools, causing jagged wounds. Poison gas was also used. The young women conducting a hunger strike on the square "for sovereignty" suffered most heavily. Twenty-one people were killed or mortally wounded in this massacre, among them sixteen young women. Most of the dead had suffered damage to their lungs from poison gas; two had no marks of external injuries, and poison gas was apparently the sole cause of their deaths.

Academician Tamaz Gamkrelidze, who had come to Moscow from Georgia for the Academy's election of deputies, asked me to join a Public Commission that had been formed in Georgia to investigate the events of April 9. I agreed. Soon I received word that patients in Tbilisi hospitals had gone on a hunger strike, demanding that the army disclose the formula of the gas that had been used and that the Red Cross send a mission to Tbilisi.

I called Alexander Yakovlev to inform him of these requests and naturally asked who had given the order to call in the troops. Yakovlev replied that the army had been summoned by Dzhumber Patiashvili (he resigned as First Secretary of the Georgian Communist Party on April 14) and that the troops had used ordinary Cheryomukha tear gas and the more potent CS gas, which had somehow been brought to Georgia from Afghanistan. I passed along the news about the CS gas through Gamkrelidze's brother, but no one seems to have paid much attention to this information at the time.

ON MAY 3 I was invited to the Moscow City Council to attend a meeting of Moscow deputies with Party and state leaders. Gorbachev, Anatoly Lukyanov [then a Central Committee Secretary], Lev Zaikov [then Moscow Party chief], and others were present.

I spoke briefly in favor of the agenda proposed by the group of deputies who had been gathering at the House of Political Enlightenment: it called for a broad discussion of basic issues, and only afterward elections to the Supreme Soviet and of its chairman. As Vladimir Kirillov (a deputy from Voronezh) remarked on another occasion, "American cowboys shoot first and think later. We should do the opposite—think before we shoot. We've shot more than enough in the last seventy years."

I also spoke of the need to repeal the laws on demonstrations and on special troops, and of the flaws in the decrees of April 8, which were intended to replace articles 70 [anti-Soviet agitation] and 190-1 [slander of the Soviet system] of the Criminal Code. I repeated my main thesis, that it is unthinkable to allow criminal prosecution for opinion or for acts of conscience, provided there is no use or advocacy of violence. "Anti-constitutional actions" is not a precise term. (Later at the Congress I spoke on this same issue. Gorbachev objected: "Democracy must defend itself"; from my seat I retorted: "Even by anti-democratic means?")

Gorbachev reacted very negatively to my suggestions. Two economists, Popov and Shmelyov, spoke well and to the point. The latter responded acidly to a speaker who proposed creating a special police force, a new Cheka, to fight illegal unearned income and the misdeeds of cooperatives. Shmelyov observed that the ruination of the economy was due to those who control 95 percent of it, the agencies of the state. The Cheka began with a struggle against petty speculation and ended up with the mass arrests and executions of 1937. Gorbachev responded, saying that the KGB would be asked to fight racketeering.

The dramatic conclusion of the meeting was Telman Gdlyan's speech, which, however, requires some background. One consequence of the introduction of a cotton monoculture in Uzbekistan was the emergence of the "Uzbekistan mafia," a band of bribe-takers, embezzlers, and corrupt Party and state officials, headed by First Secretary Sharaf Rashidov and the sadistic Minister of Internal Affairs Yakhyayev. The main source of income for these criminals came from using inflated figures of cotton production in Uzbekistan. The fictitious output was compensation of a sort for the low prices fixed by the state: this was the only way the producers could make ends meet. But of course, the fraud was illegal and opened the door for a whole hierarchy of mafiosos on the take, who demanded their cut of the "illegal" money. The criminals must have enjoyed support at the highest levels in Moscow, otherwise they couldn't have gone unpunished for many years. The investigation of this case was assigned to Gdlyan, a senior investigator of the USSR Procuracy, and he was assigned a large team of sleuths. According to our newspapers, their work was quite dangerous in its early stages.

Investigations in the USSR receive little supervision. They are conducted by the Procuracy, which is also responsible for overseeing the faithful execution of the laws. As a result, the investigating organs can often violate the legal code and elementary humanity with impunity. Testimony is extracted through barbarous means. In political cases, which attract public attention, abuses are less common, but they do occur. One can assume that Gdlyan's transgressions were in proportion to his extraordinary powers.

Public interest in Gdlyan's work was piqued when *Ogonyok* reported not long before the Nineteenth Party Conference that his group had uncovered evidence implicating highly placed Moscow protectors of the

Uzbekistan mafia; this and several follow-up articles turned Gdlyan and his deputy, Nikolai Ivanov, into heroes, especially among workers.

In early April, I attended a talk at FIAN given by Olga Chaikovskaya, a staff writer of *Literaturnaya gazeta*. She told us that Gdlyan held suspects under grim conditions in an underground prison for many years: six died during the investigation and six more committed suicide. Undoubtedly, the articles praising Gdlyan had been sanctioned at the highest level, as had the violation of the maximum nine-month term for pretrial detention. At the time of her visit to FIAN, Chaikovskaya was not allowed to publish the evidence in her possession, but all that changed by the end of April. This shift in attitude may have been linked to the Central Committee Plenum that took place on April 25, at which many high-placed opponents of *perestroika* [110 full and candidate members of the Central Committee and the Central Auditing Commission] were forced to retire. If they had been blackmailed into going quietly by threats of exposure, by some sort of "gentlemen's" agreement, then Gdlyan's muckraking had served its purpose. In any event, storm clouds began to gather over Gdlyan.

When he appeared before the meeting of the Moscow deputies on May 3, he began by crying out dramatically: "I've been accused of state crimes. Look! Before you stands a state criminal!"

"It's quite possible!" Boris Pugo shouted back from the audience (he was chairman of the Party Control Commission, replacing Mikhail Solomentsev, who had been mentioned by Ivanov as "involved in the case"—a rather ambiguous phrase).

Gdlyan went on to say that a few days earlier (after the April Plenum) one of the prisoners, the former chairman of the Council of Ministers of Uzbekistan, had been visited in his cell secretly at night by USSR Procurator-General Alexander Sukharev, his deputy Alexei Vasiliev, and Colonel Dukhanin of the KGB. The next morning, he retracted a substantial part of his earlier testimony concerning payment of large bribes to highly placed people in Moscow. Gdlyan went on: "I have documents which prove that crimes were committed by top Party and state officials. Meet with me, Mikhail Sergeyevich [Gorbachev], so that I can show you the evidence. I ask you to appoint a special commission of People's Deputies to examine the charges against me. I don't trust any other commission, and I won't testify before any other."

Gorbachev listened without interrupting. Then he said with a grim expression, "This is an extremely serious matter. I'll see you, but if you can't prove your charges, I don't envy you."

THE NEXT DAY Lusia and I flew to Tbilisi, where we moved into the apartment over the Kura River that I mentioned earlier. To the right we could see the Metekhsk Castle perched on a cliff over the water. Before the revolution, Lusia's father, Gevork Alikhanov, had been incarcerated in that stronghold. He managed to escape by lowering himself on a rope into a boat waiting below. The Bolsheviks really were daredevils. But today the whole country stands on the brink of a much more terrible precipice.

In Tbilisi, we attended a joint session of the Public Commission and the Commission of the Georgian Supreme Soviet on the events of April 9. An ambulance doctor testified that soldiers pulled a pregnant nurse out of an ambulance (marked with a Red Cross, of course) and beat her to death. She was not even a participant in the demonstration—she was just there in case someone needed medical attention. The woman's mother died of a heart attack the day she learned of her daughter's death.

An Afghanistan veteran who was present at the slaughter in the square told us that one soldier tried to save two young women by carrying them away from the field of action. An officer shouted at him: "Come back here, Andreyevsky!" The soldier returned to his unit, where he was immediately knocked down and beaten.

The Georgian Minister of Internal Affairs said that he had opposed calling in troops and had offered to handle the situation with his own forces. But Dzhumber Patiashvili and his deputies, including Boris Nikolsky (the Second Secretary—in all Union Republics this post is held by "Moscow's man"), did not agree.

We visited one hospital where many victims of gas poisoning and beatings (aggravated in some cases by psychological factors) were in serious condition. We entered the room of a severely injured young woman on an intravenous drip. The doctor told us her story. She regained consciousness after she had been knocked senseless by the soldiers, and began to crawl away from them. They shouted, "You're still alive, you bitch!" and began kicking her, especially in the stomach. One of the soldiers opened a gas canister right next to her face.

In the hospital we also met with students who were conducting a hunger strike as surrogates for the patients. They were threatening to extend the sympathy strike to other cities in Georgia, but we persuaded the patients and the students to end the strike, promising to do everything possible to support their demands, and in particular to expedite the arrival of Western doctors.

At Lusia's suggestion, I called the U.S. Embassy in Moscow and asked Ambassador Jack Matlock to send us data about CS gas; two days later, we received the information. Lusia knew French doctors from Médecins sans Frontières, who travel to all parts of the world to care for the victims of disasters, and we got in touch with them through Irina Alberti. I called Shevardnadze's assistant at the Ministry of Foreign Affairs, and he promised to expedite their visas. Of course, things never go smoothly in our bureaucratic world, and Lusia had to call Irina, the Ministry, and the Georgian mission in Moscow many more times. It was equally difficult to organize a visit by American doctors (their team included skilled toxicologists). The arrival of these two groups (a mission from the International Committee of the Red Cross managed to get to Tbilisi without requiring any assistance from us) calmed the Georgians and eased the atmosphere. The American doctors confirmed the use of gas, probably including chloropicrin in addition to those mentioned earlier.

Before our departure from Tbilisi, we met separately with Patriarch Ilya and Givi Gumbaridze, Patiashvili's replacement as First Secretary. I asked the patriarch if the report was true (Gorbachev had repeated it on May 3) that when he came to the square to ask people to disperse they insulted him. The patriarch denied this categorically.

I asked Gumbaridze who was responsible for the tragic turn taken by the events of April 9. He replied, "Read the materials of the Plenum." He was speaking of the April Plenum of the Central Committee and was implying that the conservatives who were now retired had been responsible. At the time his answer struck me as sincere, but things no longer seem that simple.

BACK IN MOSCOW, our pre-Congress caucuses continued. I was elected a "representative"—one-fifth of all the People's Deputies were to meet and discuss the Congress agenda prior to its official opening. Right up to the last day it wasn't clear when this session would take place, and the confusion led me to cancel a long-planned trip to France for a conference on the violations of CP-invariance. My attendance, even for a day, would have been a sign of respect for the French scientists who had invited me and who had defended me vigorously in my Gorky exile. Later, of course, it turned out that the bureaucracy had conveniently forgotten about us and our planning session, and had completed their own draft of the agenda, which made the election of the Chairman of the Supreme Soviet the first order of business.

Before the Congress opened, I was approached by Academician Vladimir Kudryavtsev, director of the Institute of State and Law, who told me that he was a member of the Supreme Soviet's commission investigating the allegations of serious violations committed by Gdlyan. I asked, "Did he beat the suspects?"

"No, there was nothing like that. But he unlawfully extended the term of pretrial detention, and there were other serious infractions. Gdlyan hasn't been able to support many of the charges he made. I want you to be aware of this. Our commission will probably be dissolved and another one composed of deputies appointed." Kudryavtsev made no concrete proposal, but was evidently sounding me out.

ON MAY 19 I flew to Syktyvkar (capital of the Komi Autonomous Republic) in order to campaign for Revolt Pimenov, a defendant at the first dissident trial I'd attended nineteen years earlier. After serving his term of exile, Pimenov remained in Syktyvkar, working as a mathematician. He was now in a runoff election for deputy. I appeared at several well-attended meetings, including one at the biggest factory in town. I was asked many questions, and not just about Pimenov. In fact, interest focused on Gdlyan's suspension, the allegations against him, and their potential effect on the bribery investigation.

I taped a statement on Pimenov's behalf to be shown on television, but it wasn't broadcast, probably on the orders of Vladimir Melnikov, the region's conservative First Secretary.

Pimenov lost the runoff two days later. He received a substantial majority in Syktyvkar, but the rural precincts went for his rival, and it's at least possible that my television spot, if shown, might have made a difference.

* * *

WHILE IN SYKTYVKAR, I was naturally asked my opinion of Gorbachev and Yeltsin. I just can't see an alternative to Gorbachev at this critical juncture. Even though his actions may have been prompted by historical circumstances, it has been Gorbachev's initiatives that have completely altered the country and the psychology of its people in just four years. At the same time, I don't idealize him, and I don't believe he's doing all that's needed. Furthermore, I think it's extremely dangerous to concentrate unlimited power in the hands of a single man. But none of this changes the fact that there is no alternative to Gorbachev. I have repeated these words many times in many places—Gorbachev's face lit up with joy and triumph when I said them once again at the pre-Congress planning session.

Now, about Yeltsin. I respect him, but he is a person of a different caliber than Gorbachev. Yeltsin's popularity is to some extent dependent on Gorbachev's "unpopularity," since Yeltsin is regarded as the opposition to, and victim of, the existing regime. This is the main explanation of his phenomenal success (five or six million votes, 87 percent of the total) in the elections for deputy from the city of Moscow.

Yeltsin took part in the work of the group that met at the House of Political Enlightenment. Most of the time he kept silent, but his infrequent remarks were on target, and he may have played a role in having the Congress sessions televised live, without editing. Gorbachev promised to arrange this when he met with the Moscow deputies on May 3. At a later meeting in the presence of Lukyanov and Lev Zaikov [then First Secretary of the Moscow Party organization], Yeltsin got up and said, "In the television and radio listings for next week, there's nothing about live coverage from the Congress. Only daily wrap-ups and interviews with deputies are scheduled. They're trying to trick us and the whole country. Whoever's at fault should be punished. The State Committee for Broadcasting must correct the error." Lukyanov began placing calls on several different phones. The next day he assured us that the mistake had been rectified.

On May 21 there was a big rally at Luzhniki. The initiative for the meeting came from the Moscow Tribune—more specifically, from Leonid Batkin, if memory serves. The purpose, as the organizers saw it, was to respond to the events in Tbilisi, which were seen as the reactionaries' attempt to impose their own "rules of the game." In fact, the whole program was overtaken by events. I had agreed to take part (even though Lusia thought it was a bad idea). Yeltsin and Gdlyan were also there. Before the speeches began, Gdlyan came up to me and said how pleased he was to meet me in person. I told him that I wasn't at all convinced of the truth of the accusations lodged against him, but I was just as dubious about his own allegations. Gdlyan's face darkened and he walked away.

At my request, I was third on Batkin's list of speakers. A worker from a Moscow factory was to speak first, followed by someone from the Initiative Group. But the worker didn't show up, and just at that moment Yeltsin appeared on the podium. Batkin and the other organizers consulted together in front of the microphone, and then asked him to open the meeting. Yeltsin talked about our draft agenda for the Congress and made it seem that he somehow represented the Moscow Group. Many people got the impression that the rally had been organized in support of Yeltsin. I had planned to speak myself about the agenda, and after Yeltsin preempted many of my points I had difficulty recasting my speech, so that it fell rather flat.

May 21 is my birthday, but the mood had been spoiled. Lusia said, "You should have listened to me. We could have flown to Paris for the day. The physicists had a special cake baked for you, and you've hurt their feelings."

Two other rallies in Luzhniki were much more successful. Two hundred thousand people assembled there on May 28, and I had an opportunity to rehearse my first speech to the Congress.

7

THE CONGRESS

AND SO the Congress! It convened May 25 at 10 A.M. in the Great Kremlin Palace. Delegates were seated according to their districts, and alphabetically within each territorial group. Next to me was Galina Semyonova, editor of the magazine *Peasant Woman*. She kept up a running commentary on the speeches—"Come on, sweetie, what are you saying!" She called me "sweetie" sometimes, too. I had been up since six that morning, mulling over whether I should speak and what I should say. I hadn't written anything down, which was a mistake. Later I saw that all the other speakers were reading from prepared texts, and I followed their example for my speech on the last day of the conference.

From its first minutes, the Congress took on an extremely dramatic character. The Latvian deputy V. F. Tolpezhnikov proposed a moment of silence in memory of the dead in Tbilisi (everyone rose) and then put a question: "I want to know who gave the order to beat peaceful demonstrators in Tbilisi and to use poison gas against them." No answer was ever given.

After the proposed agenda, based on the Presidium's draft, was read aloud, I asked for the floor. Gorbachev gave it to me immediately. From the very beginning of my speech the audience began whispering, clapping, and even shouting, and toward the end of my speech this turned into an overt attempt to drown me out. After I finished, a member of the secretariat came up to me and asked me to enter corrections into the transcript and sign it. I made two small stylistic changes. One sentence had been recorded incorrectly; since I couldn't remember exactly what I'd said, I simply crossed it out. The text published in *Izvestia* and in the Congress *Bulletin* didn't take my changes into account, but I have tried to recall them and include them in the version that follows.

Honored deputies, I want to speak in defense of two fundamental ideas which form the basis for the draft agenda produced by a group of Moscow deputies and endorsed by deputies all over the Soviet Union.

We began our work with the idea that this Congress is a major event in the history of our country. The electors and the people voted for us and sent us to this Congress to assume responsibility for the country, for the problems that are facing it, for its future course. Our Congress should not begin with elections—that would reduce it to a congress of voters. Our Congress must not yield its legislative power to one-fifth of its members.* The planned rotation makes no real difference. Moreover, according to the amendments to the Constitution that were rushed through, the rotation is set up in such fashion that only 36 percent of the deputies will have an opportunity to serve in the Supreme Soviet.

In conformity with this principle [the legislative supremacy of the Congress], the Moscow group proposes the adoption, as one of the first items on our agenda, of a Decree of the Congress of People's Deputies. We are living through a revolution, *perestroika* is a revolution, and "Decree" seems the most appropriate word in the circumstances. It should proclaim that the Congress of People's Deputies has the exclusive right to adopt laws for the USSR, and to appoint people to the highest posts of the USSR, including the Chairman of the Council of Ministers, the Chairman of the Committee of People's Control, the Chairman of the Supreme Court, the Procurator General, and the Chief Arbiter of the USSR. In connection with this, those articles of the USSR Constitution—in particular, Articles 108 and 111—which enumerate the powers of the Congress and the Supreme Soviet should be amended accordingly.

---

*There are 2,250 People's Deputies, while the combined membership of the two chambers of the Supreme Soviet is 542. Twenty percent of the members of the Supreme Soviet are to be replaced annually over the five-year term of the Congress.

The second fundamental question facing us is whether we have the right to elect the head of the state—the Chairman of the Supreme Soviet of the USSR—without debate, without a discussion of the political questions that will determine the fate of our country and that we are duty bound to examine. The established order is to present and discuss the candidates' platforms before elections are held. We will shame ourselves before all our people—that is my profound conviction—if we do otherwise. We must not allow this. [Applause.]

Many times in my speeches I have expressed my support for the candidacy of Mikhail Sergeyevich Gorbachev. [Applause.] I continue to support him, since I don't see another person who could lead our country. But such people might appear. My support is conditional. I feel that we should have discussion, we should hear a report from the candidates, keeping in mind the principle of competitive elections for all posts, including Chairman of the Supreme Soviet. The candidates should present their political platforms. Mikhail Sergeyevich Gorbachev, who was the father of *perestroika*, whose name is linked with the birth of *perestroika* and the leadership of the country for the past four years, should tell us what has happened during that time. He should speak of both accomplishments and mistakes, and not be afraid of self-criticism. And our attitude will be influenced by that. He and the other candidates should explain what they are planning to do in the immediate future to overcome the crisis that has developed in our country and what they will do later on. [At this point the noise in the hall reached a peak.]

Gorbachev: Let's agree that if anyone wants to speak to particular issues, the maximum time is five minutes. Finish up, Andrei Dmitrievich.

Sakharov: I'm almost done. I won't enumerate all the questions that need discussion. They're contained in our draft. I hope you've had a chance to look it over. [Loudly, trying to outshout the hall.] I hope that this Congress will be worthy of the great task that stands before it, that it will approach its work in a democratic spirit.

There were several fundamental issues of principle that I didn't raise—constitutional reform and the relations among the national administrative units of the Union, land ownership, a single uniform law on industrial and commercial enterprises. I assumed that these questions would be raised by other deputies, and the time limit had placed me under psychological pressure.

Gavriil Popov spoke after me. He tried to find a compromise on the agenda (based on the maxim, which he repeated, that politics is the art of the possible). The majority of the Congress, however, was not prepared for any compromise—that became clear both to the delegates and to the viewers at home.

Subsequently, the very logic of the debates and the whole course of the Congress led to radicalization of many deputies. The number voting with us on critical issues increased continually. Of course, quite a few conservative deputies couldn't be moved by any arguments or facts, but many others proved capable of revising their ideas. If the Congress had lasted another week, it's just possible that the "left" minority would have become a majority.

Much more important, a similar evolution was taking place across the entire country, where everyone remained glued to their television sets. Interest in the broadcasts was extraordinary. People watched at home and at work, and some took vacations so they could watch all day.

Wherever people gathered—in factories, in offices, on public transportation, in stores—the Congress was a topic of conversation.

What was its main political outcome? It didn't resolve the question of power, since its composition and Gorbachev's attitude made that impossible. Therefore, it couldn't lay the foundation for dealing effectively with economic, social, and environmental problems. All that is work for the future, and life is spurring us on. But the twelve days of the Congress completely demolished the illusions that had lulled everyone in our country and the rest of the world to sleep. Speeches by people from the four corners of the country, from both left and right, painted a merciless picture of what life is really like in our society—the impression in the minds of millions of people transcended anyone's personal experience, however tragic it might be, as well as the cumulative efforts of newspapers, television, literature, movies, and the other mass media in all the years of *glasnost*. The psychological and political repercussions were enormous, and they will persist. The Congress burned all bridges behind us. It became clear to everyone that we must go forward or we will be destroyed.

Lusia and I worked out a routine for the days of the Congress. In the morning I was driven to the Kremlin, to the Spassky Tower, by an Academy driver, and then walked from there in about five minutes to the Palace of Congresses. Lusia watched the proceedings on TV. (Sometimes her cousin Zora or some friend from Moscow or Leningrad would call, asking excitedly, "Did you hear what they said? What does it mean?") As soon as a break was announced, Lusia dashed to the car, drove to Spassky Tower, and waited for me at the chain that blocked off much of Red Square from everyone but deputies and officials. When I emerged, we rode to the Rossiya Hotel for lunch, and then Lusia drove me back to the Kremlin and returned to her television set. She would pick me up again at night when the session was over.

I can't retell all the events of the Congress—the transcript has been printed in the *Bulletins* of the Congress and in *Izvestia,* and every day and every speech at the Congress deserves the most careful scrutiny and analysis. I will limit myself to the more important events in which I personally participated and some incidents that occurred behind the scenes.

THE FIRST DAY of the Congress focused on the election of the Chairman of the Supreme Soviet. During a break, Alexander Yakovlev came over to me and said, "You spoke well. But now the important thing is to help Mikhail Sergeyevich. He has taken on enormous responsibility, and it's very difficult for him as a person. In effect he's turning around the whole country single-handedly. Electing him means guaranteeing *perestroika.*"

I said, "I know there's no alternative to Gorbachev, I've always said that. But now I have more reservations."

Yakovlev: "Too bad! You're greatly mistaken, and . . ."

Suddenly we were surrounded by people. Yakovlev broke off in mid-sentence and walked away.

Speaking before the Congress for the second time on opening day, I explained my position carefully, "I want to return to what I said this morning. My support for Gorbachev in today's election is conditional. It depends on the discussion of fundamental political issues. . . . We can't allow the election to be simply a formality—if that's what it becomes, I'll abstain from voting."

A few questions were put to Gorbachev, but clearly not enough, although he was pressed somewhat about his combining the roles of General Secretary of the Communist Party and Chairman of the Supreme Soviet. Gorbachev's competitors fell by the wayside: Alexander Obolensky's nomination was voted down by the "machine," and Yeltsin withdrew, explaining that he was acting in accordance with resolutions of the Nineteenth Party Conference and the May Plenum of the Central Committee.

When discussion of the electoral commission began, I rose from my seat and walked out of the hall; I felt the eyes of thousands of people on me. The next day Gorbachev asked me why I had left during the voting. I said that it was a matter of principle. "But there was a discussion." "Not what was called for."

As PETER REDDAWAY mentioned in his article "The Threat to Gorbachev" [*New York Review of Books,* Aug. 17, 1989], the Gdlyan case and the events in Tbilisi were two time bombs at the Congress, but I didn't become directly involved in either one.

Soon after the Congress opened, the president of the Uzbek Academy of Sciences came up to me and said, "The so-called Uzbek affair has been overwhelmed with falsehoods that insult and deeply wound my people. We all recognize your honesty, your authority. You should be on the commission investigating the Gdlyan case."

I replied, "I can't. It would take months for a newcomer to unravel the facts in the matter. And unless he does so, he risks compromising his own authority."

On May 26 or 27, Gdlyan came over and said, "When you left the hall rather than vote for Gorbachev, Ivanov and I wanted to join you. But we're under investigation, so we restrained ourselves."

"I'd like to ask you a few questions, if you don't mind," I countered. "They say that much of the evidence on bribery was given under duress, coerced by psychological pressure and lengthy imprisonment in inhuman conditions. And that the defendants are now repudiating their testimony."

Gdlyan: "The ones who are recanting were kept in Tashkent in deluxe conditions. They're being held in much worse circumstances right now in Moscow. The prolonged detentions were necessary, but I didn't make the final decision. Permission always came from Moscow."

(At the meeting of Moscow deputies on May 3, Gdlyan had argued in his own defense, "They say that I kept children in jail. But those children were forty years old, and it was the only way to get back the millions of the people's money that they stole.")

I asked Gdlyan his opinion of Galkin, the investigator who replaced him on the Uzbek case. Galkin had earlier stalled the investigation into the Sumgait pogrom; and apparently, if it was not his namesake, he was the investigator assigned to many dissident cases, including Yuri Shikhanovich's 1973 arrest for samizdat activity [see *Memoirs*, pp. 371–73].

"Galkin is my old friend. His fault—or misfortune—is that he doesn't know how to stand up to the authorities. I never give in to pressure."

A few hours after this conversation, a letter was passed down the row of seats to me. I opened the sealed envelope, which was addressed to Gdlyan and myself. An anonymous letter contained the name and two phone numbers of a person (I forget whether he was a chauffeur or a teacher) who allegedly could confirm the fact that Gorbachev had received 160,000 rubles in bribes while working in Stavropol. The letter also reported that Gorbachev accepted bribes from Armenian construction crews employed there and that this was widely known.

Unsigned letters that give other people's names and telephone numbers always smack of provocation. Nevertheless, I decided to pass the letter along to Gdlyan, who accepted it with an impassive expression.

On May 30, soon after my conversation with him, the Congress discussed the creation of a commission to examine "the Gdlyan affair." The Presidium nominated a long list of members, and Roy Medvedev was named chairman. I wasn't included. Then an Uzbek (Mukhtarov was his name, I think) exclaimed, "Medvedev is one of those writers, and a chairman like that can't be objective." Mukhtarov apparently wasn't aware that Medvedev's candidacy had been the subject of preliminary soundings, like mine. The chairman of the session finessed the situation, proposing that the list be discussed another time. "And the members of the commission can name their own chairman."

Two days later the list compiled by the Presidium was presented to the Congress virtually unchanged. Medvedev was named chairman again, and Mukhtarov no longer objected, but a group of deputies from

Sverdlovsk proposed an alternative list. Among others, it included Leonid Kudrin, a judge who resigned from his job and from the Party because he found the pressures exerted on the judiciary unacceptable. He was working as a truck driver and won his seat to the Congress after a fierce battle. I had wanted to propose his name for chairman of the commission the day before. Now I said:

> The Gdlyan case has two aspects. It's an inquiry into the work of Gdlyan's team of investigators, but it's also an examination of the charges made against the highest levels of the bureaucracy and our society. There is a crisis of trust in the Party and the leadership [that sentence was omitted in the transcript, but I said it]. Both sides of the question must be studied objectively. . . . The chairman of the commission should enjoy the confidence of the people, of the working class [this sentence was left out too]. A man with Kudrin's biography would make a fitting chairman, in my opinion.

The version published in the official *Bulletin* looks a bit different, with Mukhtarov opposing two journalists from the alternative list instead of Medvedev. If my version is correct, and I believe it is, then the attempt to fudge the discussion regarding Medvedev is symptomatic of other distortions in the transcript.

MAY 30 brought more surprises. The deputy from the Karakalpak Autonomous Republic,* Tulepbergen Kaipbergenov, spoke of the ecological catastrophe affecting the region of the Aral Sea, of the sand and salt from the sea's dried-out basin dumped by the wind on the land for hundreds of miles to the south, of the herbicides, pesticides, and other poisonous chemicals that were poured by the ton on each acre of Karakalpakia. The people of the Aral region are doomed. Birth defects are up sharply. Of every three people examined in the Karakalpak Republic, two have either typhoid fever, cancer of the esophagus, or hepatitis. The majority of the afflicted are children. Doctors counsel against breast-feeding infants. Kaipbergenov said:

---

*The Karakalpak Autonomous Republic has an area of 61,000 square miles and a population of more than 1,200,000. It is located south of the Aral Sea in Uzbekistan.

First, we should form a commission of deputies and grant them extraordinary powers. [This plea, like so many others at the Congress, still hangs in the air unanswered.] Second, the planting of cotton should immediately be cut back. Trading in cotton is literally trading in the health of your fellow citizens. The Aral region should be designated an ecological disaster area, and we should appeal to the world for help.

Other speeches recounted the disastrous ecological conditions in Uzbekistan, the near-extinction of the peoples of the North, the radioactive contamination of an enormous region as a consequence of the Chernobyl reactor accident, the pollution of air and water by the chemical and metallurgical industries. The environmental situation of our country is catastrophic and can be attributed in large measure to the pursuit of selfish interests by our gigantic supermonopolies and their immunity from punishment, the cause of many of our other difficulties as well.

THE CONGRESS MOVED on to the Georgian issue. The first speaker, Gamkrelidze, said:

If the guilty aren't punished, public opinion will see it as proof of the omnipotence of the Party elite and the military. The country's top leaders ought to have known in advance about an action planned on that scale and with such major political consequences.

Next to speak was Lieutenant General Igor Rodionov, commander of the Transcaucasian Military District. He insisted that violence had been in the air in Tbilisi prior to April 8, and that events there posed a serious threat to the country's stability. Rodionov denied the use of any chemical substances other than ordinary tear gas, arguing that there had been police and KGB agents in plain clothes mingling with the crowd and they hadn't been affected. Rodionov insisted that all the soldiers' actions had been defensive, taken in response to the unexpectedly strong resistance of armed extremists. "We're always harping on 1937, but things are harder now than they were in 1937. People can say whatever they like about you and you can't defend yourself." Rodionov's speech was greeted by a prolonged ovation, with many deputies and invited guests standing up to applaud. Others shouted, "Shame!" and "Get out of the Congress!" The *Bulletin* reads simply: "prolonged applause."

One of the Congress's most dramatic moments was the speech by Patiashvili, the former First Secretary of Georgia. He said, "I did not and do not deny personal responsibility. It was considered [he did not say by whom] a big mistake that we put General Rodionov in command of the operation. But this was done after Rodionov and First Deputy Minister of Defense General Konstantin Kochetov came to see me on the morning of April 8 and told me that General Rodionov had been put in charge." [I remember that Patiashvili mentioned a call from Chebrikov in Moscow, but that's not reported in the *Bulletin.*]

Patiashvili said that he (the First Secretary of the Central Committee of Georgia!) had not known on the morning of April 7 that Rodionov and Kochetov had arrived in Tbilisi, even though the latter had been there for more than twenty-four hours. I quote from memory: "I [Patiashvili], unfortunately, did not ask who had put General Rodionov in command." Then the transcript in the *Bulletin* reads very strangely: After the words "in command" the text has dots of ellipsis and then resumes with:

> I knew that you would ask this question [it isn't clear what question]. I, unfortunately, did not ask the question, and I am asking it today. . . . When it was announced at 5 A.M. that two people had died, I convened the Party Bureau and tendered my resignation, since I felt I had lost the right to head the Party organization. At that time I had no suspicion that shovels and gas had been used as weapons. Speaking frankly, if I had known about that, I would never have resigned. I would almost certainly have received a more severe punishment, but I wouldn't have retired voluntarily. . . . Comrade Rodionov categorically denied that shovels were used. Even after members of the Politburo arrived in Georgia, the comrades wouldn't admit it, and they changed their story only after three days. [The central press and television initially reported that people had died in the crush.] And it wasn't until later on in April that they confessed to the use of gas. The "Vremya" newscast was wrong when it reported that the commander refused . . .

Patiashvili was talking about the allegation that Rodionov refused to head the operation. The transcript at this point becomes indecipherable, but the scene at the Congress was unforgettable. Ending his speech in great emotional distress, Patiashvili evidently decided to make some sort of important revelation. But the audience, especially the right wing, was calling out insulting questions and trying to shut him up. The psychological pressure forced him to leave the rostrum. He walked a few steps, halted in apparent torment and confusion, and turned back. The noise in the hall increased to a roar. Patiashvili had almost reached the microphone when he seemed to cringe, to withdraw into himself. Then he turned and almost ran back to his seat.

The creation of a commission on the Tbilisi events was also discussed on May 30. My name was included on the list. I wrote a note to the Presidium asking to be excused since my past relations with some of the Georgian nongovernmental groups had been rather complicated. But I had another reason as well. I spoke of it in an interview on Georgian television, and President Albert Tabkhelidze of the Georgian Academy of Sciences expressed the same thought at the Congress—there was no need for a commission. What was needed was the answer to a single question: who gave the order to attack peaceful demonstrators, to use poison gas, to carry out a punitive action?

In the first few days after April 9, a rumor spread in Tbilisi that Gorbachev had called Moscow from London [where he was meeting with Prime Minister Thatcher] and had insisted on a peaceful resolution of the situation in Tbilisi. I have no way of knowing if this is true. Gorbachev himself, responding to a question on the eve of his election as Chairman of the Supreme Soviet, said nothing about it.

DURING THE CONGRESS I spoke twice on legal issues. The first time was during the discussion of Anatoly Lukyanov's nomination for Deputy Chairman of the Supreme Soviet. I said:

In the course of the last year a number of laws and decrees have been adopted that are causing great public concern. We don't really know who drafts these laws or how the legislative process works in general. Many lawyers have stated in writing that they don't understand at what stage and in what agencies laws are given their final form.

The 1988 decrees on demonstrations and on the duties and rights of the special forces when engaged in preserving public order are, in my opinion, a step backward in the democratization of our country and contradict the international obligations assumed by our state. They reflect a fear of the people, a fear of free democratic activity, and they have already led to skirmishes in Minsk, in the Crimean village of Lenino, in Krasnoyarsk, in Kuropaty and many other places, and to the tragic explosion in Tbilisi, which has been discussed here. I would like to know what role comrade Lukyanov played in drafting these decrees, whether he approved them, and his personal opinion of the decrees. That's my first question.

My second question concerns the decree of the Presidium of the Supreme Soviet of April 8 [on state crimes]. In my opinion, it also contradicts democratic principles. A very important idea was incorporated in the 1948 Universal Declaration of Human Rights and promoted by organizations such as Amnesty International: acts of conscience that do not involve violence or calls for violence ought not to become the subject of criminal prosecution. This principle is the cornerstone of a democratic legal system. But the element of "violence" has been omitted from the April 8 decree's definition of criminal subversion. That is why I find it unsatisfactory. And that decree also contains the notorious Article 11-1 [defamation of the Soviet system]. Unfortunately, the decree has already been applied, individuals have been tried under it, and the Plenum of the Supreme Court has issued a commentary on it (which strikes me as incomplete and unsatisfactory). It's unfortunate when a law or a decree requires external clarification, when it permits differing interpretations.

I'm discussing this issue at the insistence of many voters, and so I have the right to speak of it at this time. But here's my question to Comrade Lukyanov—what's his opinion of the April 8 decree and did he participate in drafting it?

THE SECOND TIME I spoke on Rule of Law issues was during the discussion of Alexander Sukharev's candidacy for Procurator General. I asked the following questions (I'm writing from memory):

What's your position on the debate in the press about allowing defense counsel to be present from the moment charges are brought. And how do you regard the proposal to relieve the Procuracy of its investigative function, since there have been serious violations of legality and humanity, and to restrict its responsibilities to oversight of the execution of the laws. [Sukharev: "I support both suggestions."]

I've received many letters from individuals who feel they have been unjustly convicted and from relatives of convicts. They state that they've appealed to the Procuracy, submitting documents proving that the verdicts in their cases were unjust. Some of the arguments seem convincing. In all instances, the Procuracy sent a stock reply: "There is no basis for reopening the case," without any concrete analysis of the petitioner's arguments. It's been reported in the press that most often the Procuracy doesn't even request the case files for review. I received the same sort of superficial reply to my complaint concerning the conviction of my wife, Elena Bonner. [Noise in the hall.] What's your attitude toward this? [Sukharev: "The Procuracy must try to do away with such practices. My position on this is very clear and very firm."]

What's your opinion of your colleagues Katusev and Galkin? [Sukharev: "Positive."] But Katusev, with his statements that contained false information, actually provoked the events in Sumgait, or, at any rate, he made them worse. And Galkin spoiled the Sumgait investigation, the chance to expose the organizers of the pogrom and those who stood behind them. [Sukharev: "You're wrong."]

A LIST OF proposed members of a commission to draft a new constitution for the USSR was presented to the Congress; it included Gorbachev as chairman. When a discussion began, one speaker noted, "All the people on the list are members of the Communist Party. Are they going to draft a constitution or new bylaws for the Party?"

Sagdeyev nominated me for the commission, saying that this would add at least one member who wasn't in the Party. Gorbachev appealed to the audience, asking who supported the proposal. Many applauded. Without calling for a vote, Gorbachev said, "I see you approve the suggestion. Let's consider it accepted." Undoubtedly, Gorbachev wanted me on the commission and was afraid that I wouldn't get a majority of the votes cast, a requirement for inclusion on the list.

I went to the rostrum and said, "It's evident from the composition of the commission that on all issues of principle I'll be in the minority. Therefore, I can serve on the commission only if I have the right to propose alternative formulations and principles and to take issue with recommendations that I oppose."

After I sat down, one of Gorbachev's aides came over to me and asked, "Does your statement mean that you won't serve on the commission?"

"No, I'm willing to serve on the conditions I stated."

"Good. Mikhail Sergeyevich was worried."

On May 31, several deputies from the armed services approached me during the break. They said that many people had been upset by my remark in my Canadian interview that Soviet helicopters had shot at Soviet soldiers who were surrounded to prevent them from being taken prisoner. If such things had happened, the whole army would know about it. But they themselves had served in Afghanistan and had never heard anything like that. They were convinced that I had been misled. "We want to warn you that there will be a demand for a public condemnation by the Congress of your statement."

I told them that my position was perfectly clear, that I was prepared to discuss it with anyone in any form.

OVER THE COURSE of the past year I had become increasingly troubled by Gorbachev's domestic policies. The enormous gap between words and deeds in the economic, social, and political spheres has worried me greatly, and continues to do so.

In brief, economic reform is practicable only if there are changes in the character of ownership in agriculture and industry, if the Party's and state's stranglehold on power is ended and if the highway robbery practiced by the central ministries is eliminated. So far these necessary steps have not been taken.

I'm worried that the responsibility for dealing with issues of ideology has been turned over to Vadim Medvedev and Alexander Degtyarev, who are enemies of *perestroika*, and by the many retreats in securing freedom of information.

In the field of politics, I'm concerned about Gorbachev's obvious desire to obtain unlimited personal power and his consistent orientation not toward the progressive forces favoring *perestroika* but toward compliant and controllable ones, even if they are reactionary. This has been made manifest by his attitude toward the Memorial Society and his behavior at the Congress, and also in his approach to ethnic problems, where he displays a prejudice against Armenians and Balts.

I'm disturbed by the lack of real change for the better in the situation of almost all classes of society.

All these concerns led me to feel that a frank talk with Gorbachev could be important. At the start of the morning session on June 1, I went up to the dais and told Gorbachev that I would like to speak to him one on one. All day I was on pins and needles. After the evening session, I reminded one of Gorbachev's secretaries of my request; he returned a few minutes later and said that Mikhail Sergeyevich was speaking with members of the Georgian delegation, that this would take a fairly long while, and it would probably be better to postpone the conversation to the following morning. But I told him that I would wait. I took a chair and sat down next to the door to the room where Gorbachev's meeting was taking place. I could see the enormous hall of the Palace of Congresses, dimly lit and deserted except for the guards at the doors.

After half an hour or so, Gorbachev emerged—accompanied by Lukyanov, which I hadn't anticipated, but there was nothing I could do about it. Gorbachev looked tired, as did I. We moved three chairs to the corner of the stage. Gorbachev was very serious throughout the conversation. His usual smile for me—half kindly, half condescending—never once appeared on his face.

Sakharov: "Mikhail Sergeyevich, there's no need for me to tell you how serious things are in the country, how dissatisfied people are, and how everyone expects things to get even worse. There's a crisis of trust in the leadership and the Party. Your personal authority has dropped almost to zero. People can't wait any longer with nothing but promises to sustain them. A middle course in a situation like this is almost impossible. The country and you personally are at a crossroads—either accelerate the process of change to the maximum or try to retain the administrative-command system in all of its aspects. In the first case, you will have to rely on the left and you'll be able to count on the support of many brave and energetic people. In the second case, you know yourself whose support you'll have, but they will never forgive you for backing *perestroika.*"

Gorbachev: "I stand firmly for the ideas of *perestroika.* I'm tied to them forever. But I'm against running around like a chicken with its head cut off. We've seen many 'big leaps,' and the results have always been tragedy and backtracking. I know everything that's being said about me. But I'm convinced that the people will understand my policies."

Sakharov: "At the Congress we're not dealing with the main political issue—the transfer of all power to the soviets, that is, elimination of the dual power of the Party and the soviets, which now favors the former. We need a Decree on Power, which will turn over to the Congress all legislative powers and the selection of key officials. Only then will we really have government by the people and escape from the tricks of the *apparat,* which still, in actual fact, controls legislative and personnel policy. The Supreme Soviet elected by the Congress doesn't seem competent or enterprising enough to do the job required. The country will still be run by the same old people, the same system of ministries and official agencies, and the Supreme Soviet will be almost powerless."

Gorbachev: "The Congress itself can't deal with all the laws—there are just too many of them. That's why we need a Supreme Soviet that will meet regularly. But you, the Moscow Group, wanted to play at democracy, and as a result many key people didn't get elected to the Supreme Soviet, people we had planned to include in the commissions and committees. You spoiled many things, but we're trying to fix what we can, for instance, to make Popov deputy chairman of a committee. There are new people everywhere—for instance, Abalkin will be Ryzhkov's deputy."

Sakharov: "The Gdlyan affair isn't only a question of violations of the law, although that is very important, but for the people it's a question of confidence in the system, of faith in the leadership. It's too bad that Kudrin wasn't appointed chairman of the commission: he's a worker, a former judge, a former Party member. The people would have trusted him."

Lukyanov broke in at this point: "Kudrin's whole election campaign revolved around the Gdlyan affair. He can't be impartial." (In fact, the Gdlyan affair was not the central issue in Kudrin's campaign.)

Sakharov: "I'm very concerned that the only political result of the Congress will be your achievement of unlimited personal power—the '18th Brumaire'* in contemporary dress. You got this power without elections; you weren't even on the slate of candidates for the Supreme Soviet, and you became its chairman without being a member."

Gorbachev: "What's the matter, didn't you want me to be elected?"

Sakharov: "You know that's not the case, that in my opinion no alternative to you exists. But I'm talking about principles, not personalities. And besides, you're vulnerable to pressure, to blackmail by people who control the channels of information. Even now they're saying that you took bribes in Stavropol, 160,000 rubles has been mentioned. A provocation? Then they'll find something else. Only election by the people can protect you from attack."

Gorbachev: "I'm absolutely clean. And I'll never submit to blackmail—not from the right, not from the left!"

Gorbachev spoke these last words firmly, without any visible sign of irritation. And on that note our meeting ended. I didn't record it at the time, so I'm once again relying on my memory. It's certainly possible that I've made some mistake regarding the order of the subjects discussed or the precise words used, but I'm quite sure that I've reported the substance of Gorbachev's statements accurately.

Our conversation had no concrete consequences, and none could have been expected. All the same, I feel that sometimes a frank conversation is necessary—though only if there is mutual respect, of course.

THE NEXT DAY, on June 2, the attack I had been expecting took place. Sergei Chervonopisky, a Komsomol secretary from Cherkassy who had lost both legs in the fighting in Afghanistan, accused me of slander because of my remarks in Canada. Much of his speech was devoted to the problems of Afghan war veterans. But then he mentioned "cheap politicians from Georgia and the Baltics, who have been preparing their

---

*A reference to Napoleon Bonaparte's seizure of power in France in November 1799—on the 18th Brumaire according to the Revolutionary calendar.

storm troops for a long time" and recalled "vicious insults to our brave
men on the TV program 'Vzglyad' and the irresponsible statements of
Deputy Sakharov." He read a statement denouncing my Canadian interview—it had been sent in by a group of paratroopers, and Chervonopisky
added his name to it. He ended by saying, "There are three things that
we all must fight to protect: state power, our motherland, and Communism." (The transcript reads: "Applause. All rise.")

As for me, I wouldn't lump those three words together. "I love my
native land, but with a strange love," wrote Lermontov. I think that the
conjunction of state power and Communism is unacceptable, and should
be so even for a sincere Communist.

As Chervonopisky was finishing his speech, I made my way to the
rostrum to answer his charges. My very first words elicited what the
Bulletin discreetly calls "noise in the hall." I said:

> The last thing I wanted to do was to insult the Soviet Army.
> . . . The real issue is that the war in Afghanistan was itself a crime,
> an illegal adventure, and we don't know who was responsible for it.
> I spoke out against sending Soviet troops to Afghanistan and for
> that I was exiled to Gorky. . . . And second, the focus of the
> interview was not at all as reported—we were discussing the return
> of Soviet prisoners of war from Pakistan. I stated that the only way
> to solve this problem is through direct negotiations with the Afghan
> guerrillas, through an exchange, through recognition of the guerril-
> las as a belligerent party. I mentioned reports that were known to
> me from foreign radio broadcasts: about shootings "with the pur-
> pose of excluding capture"—that was the wording used in the letter
> I recently received. [Unfortunately, I failed to explain at this point
> that I was talking about a letter that had been signed by many of
> the officers who were delegates to the Congress, including General
> Gromov, the former commander of the Soviet army in Afghanistan.
> It was addressed to the Presidium and had been passed on to me
> by the Secretariat. It demanded condemnation by the Congress of
> my Canadian interview and contained the words "with the purpose
> of excluding capture."] The style alone is convincing evidence that
> this phrase was copied from secret orders. I was insulting neither
> the Soviet Army nor the Soviet soldier; I was accusing those who

gave the criminal order to send Soviet troops into Afghanistan. [My two last sentences are garbled in the transcript.]

The official *Bulletin* reports applause and noise in the hall at this point. What actually happened was five minutes of hysteria in front of millions of viewers. The majority of the deputies and guests jumped from their seats, stamping their feet and shouting, "Shame! Away with Sakharov!" while a minority applauded.

Other speeches denouncing me followed, obviously a planned campaign. Tursun Kazakova, a high school teacher from Gazalkent, said, "Comrade Sakharov. With that one act you canceled out all your achievements. You have insulted the whole army, the whole people, all those who died. You have been disgraced in the eyes of the whole world." (Applause.)

At the close of the session, I went up to Gorbachev. He said, with evident irritation, "It's a shame you talked so much." I said, "I insist on having the floor to discuss your report." Gorbachev looked at me in surprise and then asked in a matter-of-fact manner, "Are you on the list?" "Yes, I signed up a long time ago."

I went outside. Lusia was waiting for me, as usual, at the Spassky Tower. She said, "You spoke badly, of course, but you're a real hero. I was worried only for a minute, while you were walking to the rostrum. But when you turned around and I saw your face, I calmed down immediately." As for me, I was much less upset than I had been the first day. Even though I was discomfited by the lack of documentary evidence (I still haven't discovered any), I was convinced that morally I was in the right, so the noise and jeers didn't bother me. All who were present in the hall or watched on TV were profoundly affected by the scene. In one hour I gained the support of millions of people, a popularity I had never before enjoyed in our country. The Presidium of the Congress, all the mass media, FIAN, and the Presidium of the Academy received tens of thousands of telegrams and letters in support of Sakharov. Our telephone kept on ringing around the clock, the mailman (with whom we're on excellent terms) had to work overtime, burying us under mounds of letters.

*   *   *

THERE WAS only one week left before the scheduled end of the Congress. Many of us thought the session should be extended, but apparently Gorbachev and the rest of the Presidium disagreed with us. Moreover, the Congress had lost a day, when we canceled our deliberations to mourn the victims of a terrible catastrophe—two trains were derailed and hundreds of passengers died when a gas line exploded in Bashkiria.

On the same day [June 4], the Chinese government used its army to crush the students and workers who had been peacefully demonstrating in Tiananmen Square for democracy and freedom of speech. We don't know the number killed in Beijing and elsewhere, but undoubtedly there were thousands of victims.

Yesterday [August 3, 1989] at Efrem and Tanya's house in Newton, I met with Shen Tong, who had headed the student negotiations with the Chinese government; Lui Yan, one of the hunger strikers in Tiananmen Square; and some people from Boston's China Information Center. Shen told us that the students had called for two things—the legalization of an independent student organization and permission to publish in one of the Beijing newspapers. The authorities had rejected these demands, since they saw them as an attempt to create a new party. Martial law had been imposed on May 20, immediately after Gorbachev's visit to Beijing ended. There were 3,600 hunger strikers, most of them young women. About 120,000 people had been jailed, and arrests were continuing. Some were sent for reeducation in remote areas, others to camps and prisons. A friend of Lui's spent nine months in solitary confinement in a cell where he could only crouch.

Shen called for international sanctions of two kinds. The first kind should have the immediate purpose of stopping arrests and executions. The second should be designed to promote democratization in China. They should target the state sector of the economy and the central government, but not the private sector or the periphery. Some sanctions have indeed been imposed, but to date their effectiveness has been limited by the Soviet Union's refusal to participate. The students were anxious to hear about the situation in the USSR: Gorbachev's role, the miners' strikes, the prospects for democracy and economic reform. Both Lusia and I liked our guests very much; they were serious, dedicated, and pleasant in appearance and manner. Lui is nineteen and Shen twenty-one.

* * *

IMMEDIATELY AFTER June 4, the Congress adopted an Appeal to the Chinese People which was an empty call for a peaceful resolution of the conflict. It wasn't clear to whom the appeal was addressed: those who were using tanks and machine guns against nonviolent demonstrators or those who were trying to resist. Only a few deputies voted against the appeal, among them Galina Starovoitova. Unfortunately, I hadn't understood the shameful character of this document when it was read aloud at the Congress, but later I tried to correct my mistake as best I could. I have since been told that the appeal had been adopted at the request of the Chinese government! It was evidently needed to smooth over the political effect of the world-wide protests against the atrocities of the Chinese authorities.

IN THOSE same days there was a shocking massacre in Uzbekistan's Fergana Valley. The first meager reports made clear only that something terrible was happening. At a closed session of the Congress, Chebrikov and, I think, Vadim Bakatin, the Minister of Internal Affairs, told us much—but far from everything—about the wholesale killing. The main victims were Meskhi Turks, but Russians, Tatars, Jews, Armenians, and Ukrainians were also slaughtered. The Meskhi had lived in Georgia near the Turkish frontier until 1944, when they were deported to Uzbekistan [by Stalin, on the grounds that they supposedly were a threat to national security]. They have been stubbornly fighting to return to their homeland ever since, and in the 1960s and 1970s many of their activists were jailed.

During the pogrom in Fergana over one hundred people were killed and several hundred wounded. The murders were particularly sadistic: burning alive, crucifixion, impaling children on pitchforks, and other unspeakable horrors. Many women, and even children, were raped.

Chebrikov said that the Meskhi had been moved for their safety to a military post where they could be protected by troops. There was not enough water, no tents for shelter, and children and old people were exposed to the blazing sun. Among the instigators of the pogrom, Chebrikov named the extremist wing of Berlik, an unofficial nationalist association of the Uzbek intelligentsia; but later that accusation was dropped. The true cause of this outburst of ethnic hatred and cruelty remains completely unfathomable. But there are enough precedents—Dr. Mengele and Auschwitz, Kolyma, Cambodia, Sabra and Shatila. . . .

In any case, religious differences cannot be the motive—both the Uzbeks and the Meskhi are Sunni Muslims. Property disputes have been mentioned, and in fact the monocultivation of cotton has deprived Uzbeks of much of their farmland and doomed them to hunger. Perhaps some Meskhi had small plots of land, and the mutual support system that always exists among a persecuted minority may have made their life a hair better than that of the native population (like Jews in Europe, Russia, and the Ukraine or the Chinese in Indonesia). But if it was a question of land, then the main thrust of hatred should have been directed not toward involuntary neighbors but toward more distant and powerful enemies. We are forced to the conclusion that someone directed the crowd and channeled its hostility. A rumor was allegedly spread about that Meskhi had butchered some children in a kindergarten. That too could have been deliberate provocation, but who was responsible for it?

The day after the closed session, Lusia and I had lunch at the Hotel Rossiya as usual. Some Meskhi from Fergana were waiting at the entrance. They surrounded us and begged for help. The men wept and one woman fell to her knees. They had been detained at the train station and at the airport in Fergana and beaten by the police, and had reached Moscow only with great difficulty. The envoys said that the rioters had been aided and abetted by the local authorities—who supplied them with buses and fuel and the addresses of Meskhi (just as Armenian addresses were handed out in Sumgait).

The next day the Meskhi visited our apartment on Chkalov Street. They had met with Chebrikov the night before and asked him to arrange a meeting with Gorbachev—they couldn't leave Moscow until they saw him; it was their duty before their people.

I began calling Gorbachev's secretariat. He wasn't in, but I asked the secretary to get in touch with him and to tell him that in view of the extreme urgency of the situation (I mentioned several previously unknown facts), I was urging Gorbachev to meet with the Meskhi delegation, and I gave the secretary a list of their names. A half hour later the secretary called back and said that Mikhail Sergeyevich couldn't receive them since he was preparing for a trip to Germany. I blew up, probably as angry as I'd ever been, and shouted, "Tell Mikhail Sergeyevich that he's not going anywhere. I'll appeal to Kohl to put off Gorbachev's visit. It's impossible to receive the head of a state that permits genocide!"

For a moment, there was silence at the other end, and then the secretary said, "Wait. I'll call back." Twenty minutes later he did so and said that Ryzhkov would see the Meskhi.

That evening the delegation returned. They reported indignantly that Ryzhkov had informed them of a plan to evacuate the Meskhi from Uzbekistan to the Smolensk region and other places in Russia proper, where homes were being prepared for them. "But that's a second exile! We've been trying to return to our homeland for decades, and we're ready to give up our lives for that. If we agree to move to Russia now, we'll never get back to Georgia, we understand that all too clearly!"

Lusia and I tried to convince them that the first priority was to save lives. They couldn't refuse evacuation from Uzbekistan, because that would lead to new victims. From Russia, they could continue their battle for a return to their homeland, and one day they would achieve their goal. The Meskhi didn't agree with us and left our apartment in a huff.

I spoke with many Georgians about the return of the Meskhi to Georgia, but they had the same inflexible attitude that they exhibited in discussions on Abkhazia and Ossetia.* Later, after the Congress, I spoke with Lukyanov about the Meskhi during the conversation I describe at the end of this book. Lukyanov said that he had tried to persuade Gumbaridze to let the Meskhi return to Georgia, but Gumbaridze declared that in the present circumstances, with arable land in short supply (because of mud slides and so on) and with already tense interethnic relations, this would lead to a civil war.

Another sidelight on events in Fergana, although I can't vouch for its accuracy: I was told that in the videotapes made of the bloody events in Uzbekistan people had recognized in the crazed crowd agents of the Armenian KGB, who had been hurriedly summoned to Moscow a few days before the events. If true, this suggests the participation of the KGB

---

*The Abkhazian and Ossetian minorities have complained of mistreatment by the Georgians and have asked for transfer of their autonomous regions to the Russian Republic.

in the provocation in Fergana, but such reports must be treated with great caution.

TOWARD THE END of the Congress, the Presidium of the Congress proposed a list of candidates for a Committee of Constitutional Oversight; this was their way of pushing the creation of such a committee. A number of deputies, particularly from the Baltics, argued against any discussion of this question, since the functions and powers of such a committee were nowhere defined. In particular, there was the apprehension that such a body might interfere in the legislative activity of the Union Republics. The debate was very heated. A number of deputies walked out of the hall (I think it was the Lithuanian delegation, but the group may have included deputies from the other Baltic republics as well). The Presidium had to yield and put off discussion of the Committee of Constitutional Oversight. [The committee was in fact formed during the Congress's December 1989 session.]

A few of the left deputies managed to address the Congress on their programs: Bunich and Vlasov on May 31; Chernichenko on June 1; Shmelyov, Emelyanov, and Yablokov on June 8. I spoke on the closing day.

In order to show that left deputies have offered constructive suggestions, despite allegations to the contrary, I shall summarize a few of the more significant speeches, since they are not readily available elsewhere.

Pavel Bunich complained that our economic reforms have been only cosmetic so far, and now we're being pulled backward by a wave of retrograde measures, for instance, the attempt to legislate a norm fixing the ratio between increases in productivity and the average wage and the harassment of cooperatives by means of punitive regulation. Today, enterprises operating at a loss pay the same salaries as profitable ones. We are spending our children's money—we are living better than we work, even though we live badly. Socialism isn't simply a welfare system. Full economic accountability *(khozraschet)* should enable everyone to keep what he earns, minus taxes. If a bride leaves her husband for someone else, the hidden vices of the bridegroom are usually at fault (Bunich was alluding to the exodus from the state sector to cooperatives).

Yuri Chernichenko began with a humorous reference to the indignation against the Muscovites expressed by the "obedient majority," recalling the "charming deputy from Kazakhstan, who has deprived them of her feminine companionship" (she had said that she was afraid to sit beside the delegates from Moscow). A car doesn't go by itself, the driver makes it go. Divide-and-conquer won't work anymore. If you want to rule productively, let's unite and accomplish something! Our patience is exhausted. A farm system based on compulsion will never feed the people. The root causes of poverty and the devastation of the land are solely political. Stalinism in agriculture is an economic Vendée.* We produce six times more ore than the United States and six times less plastic. We produce ten times as many harvesters and half as much wheat. Yuri Osipian [a physicist and member of the Presidential Council] has to use an abacus for his scientific calculations. A system left to our stunted ruble and to a bureaucracy that rules without accountability will lead only to national humiliation. We are shamed by our export of 200 million tons of oil, most of it unrefined. What on earth will I leave to my grandson? We are shamed by our import of things that we could grow on our own lands, of products that can be manufactured without using up irreplaceable resources. Why do we buy 21 million tons of grain when the country produces twice as much wheat as it needs? If Murakhovsky† had paid his countrymen the billions of rubles we've spent in this fashion abroad over the last twenty-five years, we could have grown everything we needed at home in the USSR. I believe in compromise. I want to entice people away from demonstrating, dissuade them from striking. I want to repeat Lenin's most revolutionary words after "All Power to the Soviets"—"From food quotas to a food tax."‡ Without a law on the ownership and use of land, we're just spinning our wheels. No one will trust us.

Nikolai Shmelyov confessed his fears that we will face inflation, severe shortages of consumer goods, and large budget deficits for the next two or three years. If there is a crash, we can expect rationing, devaluation

---

*From 1793 to 1795, the Vendée region of western France was the scene of particularly bloody fighting between conservative peasants and the Revolutionary government.

†In November 1985, Gorbachev created Gosagroprom, a super-ministry (now defunct) charged with responsibility for agriculture and related industries. He appointed as its head his long-time associate Vsevolod Murakhovsky.

‡The key measure of the New Economic Policy instituted by Lenin in 1921 was the substitution of a tax in kind on the peasants' production for the previous policy of forcible requisitions of grain.

of the ruble, a mushrooming of the black market and the shadow economy, and a mandatory return to stern administrative-command discipline for an extended period. [Abalkin and some others seem to feel that the time to impose stricter controls has already arrived or is coming soon.—A.S.] It's unfair to make the culprit for all this the rapid increase in salaries. The degree of exploitation of our work force is the highest for any industrialized country. Wages represent only 37–38 percent of our gross national product—for the rest of the developed world that figure is 70 percent and over. Our working class is striving to increase its share of the pie, and it has every right to do that. This process cannot be stopped. Anyone who tries to blame cooperatives for the exploitation of labor is ignorant, because they turn frozen assets into useful money. The annual income of the whole population is 430 billion rubles. The cooperatives' portion of that in 1988 was about 0.25 percent (one billion rubles), so they are hardly responsible for the fact that the presses are working overtime printing new money. Apart from the problems we have inherited from the past, we have made four major mistakes in recent years: (1) the completely bungled anti-alcohol campaign; (2) the 1986 campaign against unearned income; (3) cutting back the import of consumer goods rather than machinery and grain when the price of oil fell; (4) increasing our capital investments.

Shmelyov proposed a set of measures designed to help us avert bankruptcy:

> We should return to the normal sale of alcoholic beverages (now, half the alcohol consumed is moonshine distilled from sugar). People drink out of boredom and idleness, in reaction to the fraud that surrounds them.
>
> We need to eliminate the overhang of 150 billion surplus rubles in the hands of consumers that distorts our market. To accomplish this, we need to import $15 billion worth of consumer goods as a one-time shot in the arm, plus another $5–6 billion annually for the next two or three years to achieve a balance between supply and demand. In all, about $30 billion. Where can we get that money? In the first place, we should cut back our import of grain and allow our farmers to sell part of their production for hard currency with the right to spend it as they wish. Our people aren't greedy. There's

no need to pay them the $200 a ton it costs us on the world market; they'll settle for $75. Second, we should stop importing equipment for all our gigantic construction projects for five to ten years. Third, we should look closely at our expenditures in Latin America, which according to U.S. estimates (the only ones available), cost us $6–8 billion annually. And the final source is international credits. In today's world, there's no need to repay principal, and any one of the first three sources I named will be sufficient to service the debt. Of course, in order to correct the current oversupply of money, the rubles the government receives from the sale of these special consumer imports must be written off and destroyed.

We must sell land or rent it on a permanent basis to anyone who wants it.

Talk won't do it—we must actually sell apartments, trucks, tractors, everything that we have in our warehouses.

We must sell shares in joint ventures, common stocks, and thirty-year government bonds with high yields.

The government is bankrupt. We can afford to invest only in things that will help to satisfy consumer demand in the near term.

We have invented a ridiculous and counterproductive system of agricultural subsidies. We pay someone who works well one ruble per pound of production and someone who works badly two rubles per pound of production. This must be changed!

ALEXEI EMELYANOV spoke of power and the role of the Party. The Party is often termed a guarantor of *perestroika*, but the people didn't stumble into this crisis on their own: they were led there by the Party. A one-party system is a monopolization of power, and holding two posts simultaneously, one in the Party and one in the government, is monopoly squared. We may have to accept temporarily a single person combining the posts of General Secretary and President, but it mustn't be turned into a general practice and should be banned at lower levels. We must decide as a matter of principle to eliminate all special privileges. We have never had and still do not have a political defense mechanism to ensure democracy in our country, and therefore we do not have a guarantee of *perestroika*'s irreversibility. In restructuring we should proceed from the bottom up. Each level of management should have only those functions and the minimum number of personnel necessary to service and direct its subordinates.

ACADEMICIAN ALEXEI YABLOKOV, a biologist, reported that 20 percent of the population lives in ecological disaster conditions, and another 35–40 percent in unsatisfactory conditions. Every third person living in these heavily polluted regions develops cancer sometime during his lifetime. Infant mortality in certain districts is higher than in many African countries, and the average lifespan in the USSR is four to eight years less than in developed countries. One reason for our catastrophic pollution is the impotence of elected local governments. The central ministries have no economic incentive to conserve natural resources, and hence the extensive character of their exploitation. In our conditions of monopoly, each branch of industry acts without taking into account the stress placed on the environment by other enterprises. One-fifth of the sausages produced in 1987 contained a dangerous amount of chemicals, as did 42 percent of children's dairy products. In general, we lack sufficient data on environmental conditions. No independent environmental-impact studies are conducted prior to starting major construction projects. At best, at some later date, when large sums have already been spent, a sufficiently vigorous public initiative may halt construction that threatens the environment. But what has already been spent is gone forever. For now, experts working on environmental-impact studies have no rights, and research is conducted on a semivoluntary basis. I know this from my own experience in studying the construction of a nuclear power plant in the southern Ukraine and the Astrakhan gas-condensate facility. The Tyumen petrochemical complex still has no approved construction plans, no analysis of its technical or economic viability, and no environmental-impact studies, but the Council of Ministers has authorized financing for this facility, and the projected cost is several times greater than for the Baikal-Amur railway line.

What can we do?

Return power to elected local governments.
Make polluters pay.

Switch to technologies that don't harm the environment.
Make independent environmental-impact studies mandatory.

NOT ONLY DEPUTIES of the left but conservatives as well offered constructive suggestions; and the Congress's concluding resolution, "The Basic Directions of Domestic and Foreign Policy of the USSR," incorporated some proposals from both sides. Despite what I would regard as significant omissions, and a tendency toward abstraction, the Resolution is important as a blueprint for *perestroika,* and does contain many new and valuable provisions.

The Resolution calls for several improvements in social benefits: raising all pensions at least to the level of the minimum wage (the disabled and widows and parents of servicemen killed in the line of duty would receive the same pensions as participants in the Great Patriotic War [the official Soviet name for World War II]); a study of the possibility of increasing annual paid vacation to a minimum of twenty-four days and granting maternity leave until the youngest child is three; annual cost-of-living adjustments in pensions.

In his speech, Ryzhkov mentioned the elimination of limits on the earnings of senior citizens receiving pensions. Either I misunderstood him or there were second thoughts on the subject, but the draft of the concluding resolution restricted this concession to "pensioners, working as laborers or foremen." I submitted a note to the Presidium and the editors working on the resolution, arguing that in the interests of social justice and the state this provision should be extended to farm, professional, and service workers. Many doctors, nurses, teachers, etc., of retirement age will choose not to work if their earnings will cost them their pensions, and so society will lose the services of many skilled professionals without offsetting savings. Unfortunately, in the final text, my comments (as those of many other people, of course) were not taken into account, but at least the disabled were added.

The Resolution's economic points are very general: it sets forth the basic ideas of *perestroika* without establishing any timetable or political guarantees for their realization. Emergency economic measures, such as the ones proposed by Shmelyov, were not mentioned as such in the Resolution, but some figure indirectly. For instance, there is a proposal to sharply curtail capital investment in industry, to have a commission of the Supreme Soviet review large-scale projects that are under construction or in the planning stage. The Council of Ministers is to reduce imports of grain and other food products and to use the hard currency saved as incentives for improvements in productivity. (This is not quite what Shmelyov proposed, but it's a step in the right direction.) There is no mention at all of limiting foreign aid, allowing the free sale of apartments and the means of production, obtaining foreign credit, issuing government bonds, or ending aid to unprofitable enterprises at the expense of profitable ones (this is sometimes accomplished by paying inflated prices for their products).

The Resolution reflected many of the deputies' proposals concerning due process in criminal cases. The published text reads: "The Congress has repealed Article 11-1 and has ordered a revision of the wording of Article 7 of the Decree of April 8; it directs the Supreme Soviet to review the constitutionality of the Decree on Demonstrations and the Decree on the Internal Troops of the MVD." The Resolution also mentions a changeover to trial by jury and admission of defense counsel from the beginning of an investigation. Shifting criminal investigations away from the Procuracy is not mentioned, but it does call for the elimination of improper influence by government agencies.

The constitutional structure of the Union is discussed in a general way (too general, for my taste), with reference to "Leninist principles of federation" and the "economic autonomy of the Republics and regions in conjunction with active participation in a Union-wide division of labor." This could be understood as full Republican and regional economic accountability if you read the second half of the formula as simply a recommendation for voluntary cooperation based on self-interest.

The Resolution specifically confirms that in the USSR all state power belongs to the people and is exercised through the Soviets of People's Deputies. However, with respect to the separation of the functions of the Supreme Soviet and the Congress, it rejects the notion that the Congress should have the exclusive right to pass laws (except for one-time and short-term laws) and to nominate candidates for important posts. It also fails to meet the demand of many deputies for an end to the subordination of the soviets to Party organs, for repeal of Article 6 of the Constitution [on the leading role of the Party], and for a ban on combining the posts of chairman of a soviet and secretary of a Party committee (a temporary exception could have been made, of course, for the chairman of the Supreme Soviet and General Secretary of the Communist Party). I am convinced that we must work to attain more concrete and radical decisions at the next session of the Congress.

IN THE LAST few days of the Congress, the left deputies met several times to form an Interregional Group of People's Deputies. Their caucuses usually took place in the evenings, after the working sessions of the Congress, in one of the public rooms of the Moskva Hotel, where most out-of-town deputies were staying. The discussions of the Group's manifesto were heated, but we finally arrived at a draft acceptable to everyone. About 150 deputies signed our declaration.

The Interregional Group's activities include the preparation of position papers on basic issues facing the country and the Congress, the promotion of free debate, and the coordination of deputies' efforts to institute reforms. We decided not to have a chairman or bylaws for the Group. At our last meeting before the Congress adjourned, Galina Starovoitova drafted an appeal on China which unequivocally condemned the massacre of students and workers and demanded an end to the bloodshed, in contrast to the official Congress statement that actually played into the hands of the Chinese authorities. Her appeal was signed by many members of the Interregional Group, and thus became our first joint handiwork. Lusia and I attended all the Group's meetings, we signed the appeal on China, and in my capacity as a deputy I signed the founding manifesto.

JUNE 9 WAS the last day of the Congress. After several speeches, a motion was made to end debate on Ryzhkov's report and to adopt the resolution entitled "The Basic Directions of Domestic and Foreign Policy of the USSR," subject to revision by an editorial commission. At that moment Lukyanov turned to Gorbachev and said with relief, "Well, Mikhail, that's it!" His words weren't audible in the hall, but television viewers could hear them, because the microphones were still on. (Lusia noted this, and also another, earlier remark by Lukyanov, prompting Gorbachev to change the formulation of a certain decision.) Obviously, Lukyanov felt that all the difficulties of the Congress were behind them.

But he was mistaken. The few remaining hours of the Congress saw dramatic events that altered its psychological impact and political outcome.

The deputies insisted on a continuation of the debate, but accepted a five-minute limit on speeches. A long line formed in the aisle leading to the rostrum—many delegates had not yet had any opportunity at all to address the Congress. In brief, emphatic remarks they now described the grievances of their districts, criticized specific points of the concluding document, and suggested some important amendments and additions to the sections on social problems and the economy. One of the last to approach the tribune was Vladislav Shapovalenko, the deputy from Orenburg, who read out the manifesto of the Interregional Group. Gorbachev was caught off guard; perhaps, if he'd known Shapovalenko's intention ahead of time, he'd have tried to stop him, but he hadn't expected a non-Muscovite to make this sort of mischief.

Gorbachev was obviously alarmed. He said, "Since we'll be dealing with purely internal affairs from now on, let's end the broadcast of the proceedings. Who supports the motion?"

Several hands shot up, and someone shouted, "Yes!" but the majority stared at Gorbachev in astonishment, not understanding what was happening. I rushed to the Presidium and started saying excitedly that this was a violation of . . . I couldn't remember at that moment what it was that was being violated, but later I recalled that Gorbachev himself had promised uninterrupted broadcasting of the Congress proceedings. Just at this moment the cameras were turned off, and millions of viewers saw a completely bewildered anchorwoman on the screen saying that the broadcast from the Kremlin Palace of Congresses was over (with no explanation, not even the usual "technical difficulties"). Then the transmission was switched over to the second half of a soccer match.

Apparently the broadcast had been stopped without a warning to the television center. Some disgruntled viewers turned off their TVs and went back to work or resumed their household chores. Others waited for something to happen. Zora called Lusia, who was as much in the dark as everyone else.

What had caused Gorbachev to panic? Very likely he was worried that other surprises might follow Shapovalenko's speech and that he might feel compelled to act in a manner that he would rather not have the whole world watch. In any event, he was certainly making plain his desire to keep *glasnost* within definite limits.

In his confusion, Gorbachev had evidently forgotten that he still had a pleasant surprise up his sleeve for the deputies and the public at large. Regaining his composure and seeing that there was no mutiny in the offing, he had the cameras turned back on. He then recognized Lukyanov, who announced that the Presidium, in deference to the request of many deputies, was proposing the removal of Article 11-1 from the Decree of April 8 on the grounds that the ambiguity of its operative term, "defamation," lent itself to abuse. I again rushed over to the Presidium and almost shouted, "And what about Article 7 and the principle that only actions involving violence or a call to violence can be considered criminal?"

Lukyanov smiled and said, "Wait, it's all coming. . . . The Presidium also proposes a revision of Article 7, replacing the words 'anti-constitutional acts' with the words 'violent acts.' The final text will be prepared by legal experts, but we believe that the change we suggest will satisfy everyone, even though we feel that the original wording meant the same thing." The deputies, myself included, applauded and many stood. Of course, it was necessary to show this on TV.

The Congress was coming to a close, but I persisted in my attempts to get the floor and finally, just before the final curtain, Gorbachev gave it to me. At that moment a deputy from the Theatrical Union jumped up and asked angrily why I was being allowed to speak for the umpteenth time, when the director of their organization, Kirill Lavrov, hadn't spoken even once. But Gorbachev ignored her. He tried to limit my remarks to five minutes; I demanded fifteen on the grounds that my speech would deal with issues of principle. Gorbachev refused to make this further concession.

I began speaking, with the time limit still in dispute, hoping to get my fifteen minutes through sheer stubbornness. In fact, I managed to speak for thirteen or fourteen minutes. (In order to save time, I made a few cuts while I was reading my prepared text, but I reproduce it in its entirety here.) I concluded with a plea to Gorbachev to let Starovoitova read the Appeal on China, signed by more than 120 deputies. When I saw that it wasn't in the cards, I said a few words of my own on the subject. By then Gorbachev had turned off the loudspeakers in the hall, so that only the deputies in the first few rows could hear me, but the microphones were still live and the television and radio audience heard everything I said!

I had discussed the Decree on Power with several friends, including Anatoly Shabad from the Initiative Group, but I didn't have time to check the final text of my speech with anyone, especially the first point about eliminating Article 6 of the Constitution ("The leading and guiding force of Soviet society and the nucleus of its political system, of all state and public organizations, is the Communist Party of the Soviet Union"). I probably should have included among the officials to be appointed by the Congress on the basis of competitive elections the Minister of Foreign Affairs and the Minister of Defense. I also wish I had added to the proviso on the KGB a statement that it "is forbidden to support terrorism in any form, trade in drugs, or take other actions incompatible with the principles of the new thinking [in foreign affairs]." Lusia insisted that I call for the demobilization of students drafted the year before. Whatever effect my statement in this regard may have had, these young men are now [August 1989] being processed for release from the army.

Immediately after the last session ended, someone (I think from the editorial staff of *Izvestia*) asked me to go up to the third floor of the secretariat and make corrections in the transcript. I wrote out the end of my speech in longhand, the part the stenographers couldn't hear. The head of the secretariat said that only what I had actually said on the floor of the Congress could be included. I replied that I'd said everything that I had written down. But the Congress *Bulletin* and *Izvestia* omitted the last portion of my speech, including everything on China. The version that follows is the full text.

I should first explain why I voted against the Congress's concluding document. It contains many theses that are correct and important, many ideas that are original and progressive, but, in my opinion, the Congress has failed to address the key political task facing it, the need to give substance to the slogan "All Power to the Soviets." The Congress refused to consider a Decree on Power, although a whole host of urgent economic, social, national, and ecological problems cannot be successfully solved until the question of power is decided. The Congress elected a Chairman of the USSR

Supreme Soviet [Mikhail Gorbachev] on its very first day, without a broad political discussion and without even a token alternative. In my opinion, the Congress committed a serious mistake that will significantly reduce its ability to influence national policy and that will prove to be a disservice to our Chairman-elect as well.

The Constitution now in force assigns absolute and virtually unlimited power to the Chairman of the USSR Supreme Soviet. The concentration of that much power in the hands of one man is extremely dangerous even if he is the author of *perestroika*. In particular, it opens the gate to behind-the-scenes influence. And what happens when someone else fills this post?

The construction of the state has started with the roof, which is clearly not the best way of going about things. The same approach was repeated in the elections to the Supreme Soviet. Most delegations simply appointed a slate of candidates, who were then formally endorsed by the Congress, even though many of those selected are not prepared to serve as legislators. The members of the Supreme Soviet should quit their former jobs—but only "as a rule," and this deliberately vague formula has allowed the introduction of "wedding generals" [people invited to swell the ranks at a social function] into the Supreme Soviet. I fear that such a body will simply be a screen for the real power of its Chairman and the Party-state apparatus.

We are in the throes of spreading economic catastrophe and a tragic worsening of interethnic relations; one element of the powerful and dangerous processes at work has been a general crisis of confidence in the nation's leadership. If we simply float with the current, hoping that things will gradually get better in the distant future, then the accumulating tensions could explode with dire consequences for our society.

Comrade deputies, at this moment in history, an enormous responsibility has fallen to you. Political decisions are needed in order to strengthen the power of local Soviet organs and resolve our economic, social, ecological, and ethnic problems. If the Congress of People's Deputies cannot take power into its hands here, then there is not the slightest hope for the soviets of Union Republics [the USSR is a federation of fifteen Union Republics], regions, districts, and villages. But without strong local soviets, it won't be possible to implement land reform or any agrarian policy other than nonsensical attempts to resuscitate uneconomic collective farms. Without a strong Congress and strong and independent soviets, it won't be possible to overcome the dictates of the bureaucracy, to work out and implement new laws on commercial enterprises, to fight against ecological folly.

The Congress is called upon to defend the democratic principles of popular government and thereby the irreversibility of *perestroika* and the harmonious development of our country.

Once again I appeal to the Congress to adopt the following Decree on Power:

Proceeding from the principles of popular government, the Congress of People's Deputies proclaims:

1. Article 6 of the USSR Constitution is repealed.
2. The adoption of all-Union laws is the exclusive right of the Congress of People's Deputies. USSR laws enter into force on the territory of a Union Republic after they have been confirmed by the Union Republic's highest legislative body.
3. The Supreme Soviet is a working body of the Congress.*
4. Commissions and committees charged with drafting fiscal and other legislation and with permanent oversight of state agencies and of the country's economic, social, and ecological situation shall be formed by the Congress and the Supreme Soviet on the basis of equal representation and shall be responsible to the Congress.
5. The Congress shall have the exclusive right to elect and recall the top officials of the USSR, i.e., the Chairman of the USSR Supreme Soviet, the Deputy Chairman, the Chairman of the USSR Council of Ministers [the Head of Government], the Chairman and members of the Committee of Constitutional Oversight, the Chairman of the USSR Supreme Court, the Procurator-General, the head of the State Arbitration Board, the Chairman of the Central Bank, and also the Chairman of the KGB, the Chairman of the State Committee on Television and Radio, and the editor-in-

---

*The Brezhnev Constitution defined the Supreme Soviet as "the highest body of state authority in the USSR," but in practice it served an essentially ceremonial function.

chief of *Izvestia*. The officials named above are accountable to the
Congress and not subject to decisions of the Communist Party.

6. Candidates for Deputy Chairman of the USSR Supreme Soviet and for Chairman of the USSR Council of Ministers will be
nominated by the Chairman of the Supreme Soviet, and additional
candidates can be nominated by People's Deputies. The right to
nominate candidates for the remaining posts listed in paragraph 5
is a prerogative of People's Deputies.

7. The functions of the KGB shall be limited to those necessary
for the protection of the USSR's international security.

(Provision should be made in the future for direct popular election of the Chairman of the USSR Supreme Soviet and his deputy
with nomination of competing candidates.)

I request the People's Deputies to study carefully the text of this
Decree on Power and to put it to a vote at an extraordinary session
of the Congress. I appeal to Soviet citizens to support the Decree
on Power individually and collectively, just as they supported me
when an attempt was made to discredit me and deflect attention
from the question of responsibility for the war in Afghanistan.

I would like to respond to those who are trying to intimidate you
by citing the impracticality of having two thousand persons involved in the legislative process. Commissions and committees will
prepare drafts for consideration by the Supreme Soviet, these will
then be discussed during their first and second readings, and the
transcript of all proceedings will be available to the Congress. If
necessary, debate can be continued in the Congress itself. It will
really be unacceptable if we—deputies, who have received a mandate from the people—delegate our rights and responsibilities to
one-fifth of our number [the two chambers of the Supreme Soviet],
and in actual practice to the Party-state apparatus and the Chairman of the Supreme Soviet.

Let me continue. Any danger of armed attack on the Soviet
Union vanished long ago. We have the largest army in the world,
larger than the U.S. and China combined. I suggest the establishment of a commission to prepare a draft resolution on reducing the
term of military service: the term for privates and noncommis-
sioned officers should be cut roughly in half [draftees ordinarily

serve two years], all types of weapons should be reduced accordingly, but, anticipating a transition to a professional army in the longer term, I propose a significantly less drastic reduction in the officer corps. A decision of this sort would have enormous impact internationally, building confidence and promoting disarmament (including a complete ban on nuclear weapons), as well as great economic and social significance. A particular point: all students drafted a year ago should be discharged in advance of the academic term that begins this fall.

Now to ethnic problems. We have inherited from Stalinism a constitutional structure that bears the stamp of imperial thinking and the imperial policy of "divide and rule." The smaller Union Republics and the autonomous national subdivisions, which are administratively subordinated to the Union Republics, are victims of this legacy. For decades they have been subjected to national oppression. Now these problems have come to the surface in dramatic fashion. But to an equal extent the larger ethnic groups have also been victims, and that includes the Russian people, who have had to bear the main burden of imperial ambitions and the consequences of adventurism and dogmatism in foreign and domestic policy.

Urgent measures are required to deal with acute interethnic tensions. I propose the creation of a new constitutional system based on horizontal federalism. This system would grant equal political, juridical, and economic rights to all existing national subdivisions regardless of their size or current status, and would preserve their established borders. In time, some rectification of these borders and of the composition of the federation will be possible and probably will become necessary, and this should become the main business of the Soviet of Nationalities. The Republics will enjoy equal rights, forming a union on the basis of a treaty providing for the voluntary restriction of each Republic's sovereignty only to the extent necessary for the conduct of defense, foreign affairs, and a few other matters. Differences among Republics in size of territory or population or a Republic's lack of an international frontier should not confuse the issue. Persons of different nationalities living together in one Republic should enjoy equal political, cultural, and social rights in law and in practice. The Soviet of Nationalities should be assigned the responsibility of monitoring this.

The fate of the forcibly resettled nationalities is a matter of cardinal concern. Crimean Tatars, Volga Germans, Meskhi Turks, Ingush, and others in this situation should have the opportunity to return to their homelands. The work of the commission organized by the Presidium of the Supreme Soviet to deal with the question of the Crimean Tatars has clearly been unsatisfactory.

Religious problems are closely associated with national problems. Any infringement of freedom of conscience is impermissible. It is intolerable that the Ukrainian Catholic Church has still not been officially recognized.

The most urgent political question is the confirmation of the role of the soviets and their independence. The elections of soviets at all levels must be conducted by genuinely democratic methods. The electoral law should be amended based on the experience of elections to the Congress. Regional meetings [to screen candidates] should be eliminated, and all candidates should have equal access to the mass media.

The Congress should adopt, in my opinion, a resolution embodying the principles of the Rule of Law. These principles include: freedom of speech and conscience; the possibility for private citizens and public organizations to contest before an independent tribunal the acts and decisions of all officials and government agencies; due process in trial and investigatory procedure (access to defense counsel from the very beginning of a criminal investigation; trial by jury; transfer of jurisdiction over criminal investigations from the Procurator's office, which should be solely concerned with faithful execution of the laws).

I urge that the laws on meetings and demonstrations and on the use of internal troops be reviewed, and that the Decree of April 8 [on subversion and the defamation of state organs] not be confirmed.

The Congress does not have the power instantaneously to feed the country, instantaneously to solve our nationality problems, instantaneously to eliminate the budget deficit, instantaneously to make the air and water and woods clean again, but what we are obliged to do is to establish political guarantees that these problems will be solved. *That* is what the country expects from us.

All Power to the Soviets!

Today, the attention of the whole world is riveted on China. We should take a political and moral stand on this issue that is faithful to the principles of internationalism and democracy. The resolution adopted by this Congress is not sufficient. The participants in the nonviolent democratic movement and those who initiated bloody reprisals against them are treated equally.

A group of deputies have drafted and signed an appeal, calling on the government of China to end the bloodshed. The Soviet Ambassador's presence in Beijing at this moment may be seen as tacit support by the Soviet government and people for the Chinese government's actions. In these circumstances, the recall of our ambassador is necessary. I urge that he be ordered home.

I feel that my statement was significant not only for its analysis of the facts and its specific proposals—it was important in a psychological and political sense. My speech, coming after the announcement of the Interregional Group, the defeat of the proposal to form a Committee of Constitutional Oversight, and the discussions of the two last days, helped the Congress end on a more radical, more constructive, and more inspiring note than might have been expected just a few days earlier. And that evening we felt like victors. But our triumph was tinged with a sense of the tragedy and complexity of the general situation, with an understanding of all the difficulties and dangers that lay ahead in the near term and in the more distant future. If our view of the world can be called optimism, then it is a tragic optimism.

THE NEXT DAY I went back to the Kremlin to make a contribution for the victims of the train disaster in Bashkiria and to get the Congress *Bulletins* I was missing (I failed in this). I stopped by at Lukyanov's office to find out when our Commission to Draft a New Constitution would meet. The secretary went in to Lukyanov and came back quickly to tell me that Anatoly Ivanovich would be free in a few minutes and would like to see me. Lukyanov then came out himself and escorted me into his office. It contained a bookcase filled with reference works and a large desk with telephones. A mountain landscape adorned one wall. (At the end of our conversation, Lukyanov told me that a portrait of Brezhnev had once hung there. He had put up instead a portrait of Gorbachev, but Mikhail Sergeyevich had asked him to take it down. Since Lukyanov had once been an amateur mountain climber, he had picked this painting as a replacement.)

Lukyanov said that he had great respect for me. He and Alexander Yakovlev had been the initiators of my return from Gorky. In response to my question about when the Constitutional Commission would begin work, Lukyanov replied that the plan was to hold first a Central Committee Plenum on the ethnic question, so the Commission would not be in a position to meet before September.

I said that I was going to Europe and then to the United States, where my wife and I wanted to rest and do some work while staying with her children. In particular, I wanted to think about a new Treaty of Union, a subject I had raised at the Congress.

Lukyanov replied that I could be absent until the end of August without worrying. "We're thinking about how to build our state on a country-wide scale. Naturally, there must be some form of federal structure. But at the same time we can't allow the USSR to fall apart. The forces of economic, political, cultural, and military integration are on the upswing around the world. Integration in Europe, for instance, offers great advantages in all those respects. And it would be silly if we moved in the opposite direction, toward devolution and a confederation. There are no confederations anywhere in the world now; it's not a viable form of government."

To the best of my recollection, Lukyanov didn't explain his understanding of the distinction between a federation and a confederation, and I didn't ask. But he did state that separate monetary systems, separate armies, and separate laws could not be allowed in the Union Republics.

"We've appreciated," Lukyanov went on, "your support of Mikhail Sergeyevich and *perestroika* in your speeches and articles in the years since you returned to Moscow. We follow your statements, and we thank you for them. The situation now is very complex. In April 1985, after the Plenum, Mikhail Sergeyevich and I walked all night in the woods discussing the country's problems. We clearly understood the need for far-reaching reforms and for democratization. But we didn't realize the extent of the crisis or the full measure of the difficulties ahead."

I asked him about a man condemned to death for running an underground factory in Alma Ata. I had earlier sent Lukyanov an appeal on behalf of the chief defendant, an engineer named Rozenshtein, if memory serves, who had been kept in jail in terrible conditions for eight years while his case was under investigation. He was confined on death row. His brother, an invalid since childhood, had also been imprisoned for eight years under investigation. I had mentioned this affair in a conversation with Gorbachev and Lukyanov on June 1, and the next day followed up with a note to Lukyanov in which I requested his intervention. In it I stressed that the new draft laws do not sanction the death penalty for economic crimes, and argued that executions should be suspended until the new laws have been adopted.

Now Lukyanov told me that my note had been passed on to the Legal Department of the Central Committee (his secretary gave me the phone number) and the case would be reviewed carefully. Speaking of capital punishment in general, Lukyanov said that the Presidium of the Supreme Soviet is not confirming any death sentences except those pronounced for murder involving special cruelty or multiple killings, rape leading to the death of minors, and other inhuman crimes. Not a single death sentence for economic or property crimes had been confirmed on appeal. The number of executions in the country has been reduced by eight times. (Unfortunately, I didn't ask for absolute figures.) Lukyanov questioned whether it would truly be merciful to postpone executions for crimes that would clearly incur the death penalty even under the new legislation—the anticipation of death, after all, is the most horrible part of capital punishment. He invited me to attend a few meetings of the Presidium of the Supreme Soviet when they were considering the possible granting of pardons. I agreed, reminding him, however, that I oppose the death penalty on principle.

EPILOGUE

A FEW DAYS after my conversation with Lukyanov, Lusia and I left for Europe and then the United States. This book was largely written in Newton and in Westwood, Massachusetts, in the homes of Lusia's children. She is sitting beside me, finishing work on her childhood memoirs.

Of course, completing a book gives one a sense of crossing a frontier, of finality. As Pushkin put it, "Why is this strange sadness troubling me?" At the same time, there is an awareness of the powerful flow of life, which began before us and will continue after us.

There is the miracle of science. I don't believe that we will come up with a theory that can explain everything in the universe anytime soon (and perhaps never), but I have seen fantastic advances just in the course of my own lifetime, and there is no reason to expect the stream to dry up: on the contrary, I believe it will broaden and branch out.

What lies ahead for the Soviet Union? The Congress shifted the engine of change into a higher gear. The miners' strike is something new, and it is only the first reaction to a "scissors effect," the growing disparity between expanding public awareness of our situation and the marking of time on the official level with respect to the real political, economic, social, and ethnic issues. Only a radicalization of *perestroika* can overcome the crisis without a disastrous move into reverse. The speeches of the left at the Congress marked out the rough outlines for this radicalization, but the main job still lies ahead—working together to complete the design.

How should we deal with global issues? I am convinced that their solution demands convergence—the process that has already begun of the pluralistic transformation of capitalist and socialist societies (in the USSR it's called *perestroika*). The immediate goal is the creation of a system that is efficient (which means a market and competition), socially just, and ecologically responsible.

A few words about my own family, children, and grandchildren. There is much I have failed to do, sometimes because of my natural disposition to procrastinate, sometimes because of sheer physical impossibility, sometimes because of the resistance of my daughters and son which I could not overcome. But I have never stopped thinking about this.

And finally, Lusia, my wife. Truly, she is the only person who shares my inner thoughts and feelings. Lusia prompts me to understand much that I would otherwise miss because of my restrained personality, and to act accordingly. She is a great organizer, and serves as my brain center. We are together. This gives life meaning.

INDEX

ALONE TOGETHER
by Elena Bonner

The story of Elena Bonner and Andrei Sakharov's internal exile in the Soviet Union, which "describes one of the most extraordinary struggles in history between a state and an individual—or, in this case, two individuals" (*New Republic*).

"A story of the astonishing courage of two elderly people whose hearts, though not those of adolescents, still beat strongly enough to stand up to power."

—*The New York Times*

Autobiography/0-394-75538-3/$8.95

MEMOIRS
by Andrei Sakharov

Andrei Sakharov's revealing, insightful memoirs record not only his seven years of official banishment within the Soviet Union but also recount his involvement with some of the most profound and dramatic issues and events of this century.

"Destined to take its place as one of the great testaments to human freedom in this or any age . . . a complex and brilliant blend of personal history, scientific insight, and a lesson in uncommon moral development."

—*San Francisco Chronicle*

Biography/History/0-679-73595-X/$16.00